I0017813

Computer Programming

---

2 Books in 1:

LINUX Command-Line for Beginners,

Python Programming for Beginners

---

by Dylan Mach

© Copyright 2020 by Dylan Mach - All rights reserved.

The content contained within this book may not be reproduced, duplicated or transmitted without direct written permission from the author or the publisher.

Under no circumstances will any blame or legal responsibility be held against the publisher, or author, for any damages, reparation, or monetary loss due to the information contained within this book. Either directly or indirectly.

Legal Notice:

This book is copyright protected. This book is only for personal use. You cannot amend, distribute, sell, use, quote or paraphrase any part, or the content within this book, without the consent of the author or publisher.

Disclaimer Notice:

Please note the information contained within this document is for educational and entertainment purposes only. All effort has been executed to present accurate, up to date, and reliable, complete information. No warranties of any kind are declared or implied. Readers acknowledge that the author is not engaging in the rendering of legal, financial, medical or professional advice. The content within this book has been derived from various sources. Please consult a licensed professional before attempting any techniques outlined in this book.

By reading this document, the reader agrees that under no circumstances is the author responsible for any losses, direct or indirect, which are incurred as a result of the use of the information contained within this document, including, but not limited to, — errors, omissions, or inaccuracies.

LINUX
Command-Line
for Beginners

A Comprehensive Step-by-Step Starting Guide to Learn Linux from Scratch to Bash Scripting and Shell Programming

By Dylan Mach

© Copyright 2019 by Dylan Mach - All rights reserved.

The content contained within this book may not be reproduced, duplicated or transmitted without direct written permission from the author or the publisher.

Under no circumstances will any blame or legal responsibility be held against the publisher, or author, for any damages, reparation, or monetary loss due to the information contained within this book. Either directly or indirectly.

Legal Notice:

This book is copyright protected. This book is only for personal use. You cannot amend, distribute, sell, use, quote or paraphrase any part, or the content within this book, without the consent of the author or publisher.

Disclaimer Notice:

Please note the information contained within this document is for educational and entertainment purposes only. All effort has been executed to present accurate, up to date, and reliable, complete information. No warranties of any kind are declared or implied. Readers acknowledge that the author is not engaging in the rendering of legal, financial, medical or professional advice. The content within this book has been derived from various sources. Please consult a licensed professional before attempting any techniques outlined in this book.

By reading this document, the reader agrees that under no circumstances is the author responsible for any losses, direct or indirect, which are incurred as a result of the use of the information contained within this document, including, but not limited to, — errors, omissions, or inaccuracies.

Table of Contents

5

Introduction

Congratulations on **purchasing your copy of** *LINUX Command-Line for Beginners: A Comprehensive Step-By-Step Starting Guide to Learn Linux from Scratch to Bash Scripting and Shell Programming* and thank you for doing so.

Linux is in virtually everything we use today. If you are a beginner or you are just starting to learn everything about Linux operating system, you will soon realize that downloading this eBook is a smart way into having a clear understanding of the world of Linux as well as several of its distributions. Usually, navigating through the Linux command-line can be quite tricky. In this book, you will see multiple approaches that you can model to have a smooth operation with Linux. Also, certain Linux distributions you can use not only as a beginner but also those that can function if you attempt to use it on your old system. Ultimately, this book takes a step further to analyze basic Linux shell commands as well as shell scripting.

To this end, some of the chapters in this book will discuss Linux user management and administration, where it examines some of the duties of Linux system administrator, including handling directories, users extensively, and files, basic bash commands, root, or superuser management, and so much more. Also, this book will discuss Linux file functions as well as defining the three types of Linux file ownership, permissions, and SSH commands. You will learn about other SSH commands, Linux terminals, editors, and shell.

With a clear perception of directories, file managers, and editors out of the way, this book will discuss how you can create a file for tar gzip from the command-line, how you can mount and unmounts media, and also Linux data manipulation.

On the shelves, there are several books on Linux Command-line, and for making this book your choice, we will like to appreciate the gesture. From our end, we are striving to see that this book provides you with all the practical and necessary information you will need to succeed. Once again, thank you!

Chapter 1: What is Linux and Why Using It?

Strengthening almost everything from mobile phones, servers, and PCs, Linux is a standard operating system that people commonly use. Indeed, all over the world, several individuals use Linux in all fields and applications you can imagine. Linux has been around since the 90s. From your TV stick to the fridge and everything, Linux runs everything. And much of the internet has support from Linux. Since the computer operating system has powered several innovations, many scientific breakthroughs have Linux to thank. Even though for decades, Linux has been supplying secure, reliable OS duties, the word "Linux" has no familiarity with the general public.

But Linux operating system is everywhere, from enterprise servers to home desktops, home appliances, supercomputers, cars, and smartphones. Everywhere, you will find Linux, and it is on your television, Roku devices, refrigerators, and thermostats. For being one of the stress-free, most secure and reliable operating system available, Linux prides itself as a preferred platform running embedded systems, servers, and desktops all over the world.

What is Linux OS?

In the first place, what do you understand by an OS or operating system? In a physical computer, the management of the hardware is the duty of the computer code known as the operating system. Between the hardware and software, the operating system exists as a layer. Also, in assembler, communicating with a graphics card or addressing a CPU is not what most people want to know. And what acts as a middleman is an operating system like Windows or Linux.

Therefore, Linux, like Mac OS, iOs, and Windows, is an operating system. Essentially, Linux operating system powers Android, which is the most popular platform in the world.

The software is likely not to function without the operating system since, as an operating system, Linux manages the communication between the hardware and software.

There are so many different pieces that Linux operating system comprises and they are:

- **Applications** – not all the complete array of apps that the desktop environments provide. As such, you can quickly find and install several thousands of software that are high-quality through Linux, typical of macOS and Windows. There are simplicity and centralization in the application installation by most modern Linux distributions. For example, typical of GNOME Software, there is Ubuntu Software Center by Ubuntu Linux that, from one centralized platform, speeds up the discovery and installation of apps among thousands of them for users.

- **Desktop environment** – users can interact with this piece. You can choose from several desktop environments like Xfce, KDE, Enlightenment, Pantheon, Mate, Cinnamon, GNOME, and so on. There are built-in applications for each desktop environment, including games, web browsers, configuration tools, and file managers.

- **Graphical server** – on your monitor, you will get a graphic display with this subsystem. It is known as X or X-server by many people.

- **Daemons** – after logging into the desktop or startup during boot, these are background services such as scheduling, sound, printing, and so on.

- **Init system** – user space is bootstrapped by this subsystem, and the control of daemons is in its charge. As such, systemd, as the most controversial, is an init system most widely used. When the bootloader, like Unified Bootloader or GRUB, handles the initial booting, the init system manages the boot process.

- **OS Kernel** – kernel can be referred to as a complete piece known as Linux for the management of the peripheral devices, memory, CPU, and the core of the system is the kernel.

- **Bootloader** – this software manages the process of the computer boot. It is a splash screen that pops up in the operating system and soon goes away to boot for most users.

- **OS Shell** – the shell is what we use to tell our operating system the things we want it to do. As the command line by many, you use text to instruct the OS. However, the code of command-lines is known by quite a few people. As such, this caused people to stay away from using Linux. The modern distribution of Linux changed this since, just like Windows, Linux will use a desktop.

Why Using Linux?

Most people ask this question almost all the time. When the OS that ships virtually all servers, laptops, and desktops function correctly, why would anyone bother to learn a wholly different computing environment? The answer to that question will pose another question rather than a response; are you okay with the working of your current operating system? Or are you struggling with license fees, costly repairs, crashes, slowdowns, malware, and viruses? For you, Linux may be the perfect platform if you find yourself struggling with the above. On the planet, right now, the most reliable computer ecosystem is Linux. For a desktop platform, you will have a perfect solution when you combine such the entry's zero cost with reliability. As there isn't any payment for server licensing or the software, you can have as many computers as you like to install Linux. Also, you won't have any requirement to make any payment to access Linux.

Besides that, what about having as long as you want, a stress-free, stable operating system if you are not bothered about the zero cost implications? There hasn't been an issue of viruses, malware, or ransomware by so many people using Linux, both on server platform and desktop, for more than two decades. The thing is, such attacks have no power over Linux. If only the kernel is updated, they are necessary for server reboots. And it may not be entirely out of the ordinary for a Linux server to go for years without being rebooted. You will surely enjoy dependability and stability when recommended updates are strictly followed.

Also, our computers have most of the desktop operating systems we use, and changing the operating system is something we rarely probe. What's more? Learning a new operating system is not what most people are inclined to do. However, here are some of the reasons you need to try out Linux:

A host of different distributions

There is variance in the Linux different distributions or editions. Some are for server software, while others are designed for desktop use. And while some are designed with beginners in mind, others have their focus on the advanced users. Most Linux editions otherwise referred to as distributions, use USB drive for installation, an optical disk, or can be downloaded for free. The Linux distributions are quite endless. Though some popular choices are openSUSE and Debian, the default preferences for desktop users are mostly Linux Mint, Arch, and Fedora. Courtesy of Ubuntu Unity, Ubuntu becomes one of the most modern Linux distributions. Through the inclusion of openSUSE, you can get a more traditional Linux look with KDE. Also, it is quite a long list if you are looking for the list of server Linux OS. CentOS, SUSE Enterprise, Ubuntu Server, and Red Hat are some of the most well-known distributions. However, you may need to invest in some money with the use of some Linux server distributions as licensing may be required to use Red Hat. But, quite essential for your business is the support, which you get for your license fee in return.

Linux is the same as freedom

There is a need to have the definition of an open source as equivalent to Linux. There are a set of principles that any software follows, such as:

- For any of your modified software, copies will have no restrictions

- The software distribution will have no limit

- There will be permission to make any changes needed by you, examine it, as well as study and disassemble the software

- Irrespective of your goals or motive for running it, the full freedom to run the software

Primarily, open-source software does not correlate to a community, and you need to understand that. Linux is built by this community, and Linux enjoys robust maintenance from that community. As such, people made Linux as software for the rest of the world, if you are wondering what Linux is and what has brought about the popularity of Linux. It is all about this philosophy of open source.

Linux is excellent in reliability

Since it is quite reliable, for system administrators, life is comfortable with the use of Linux. As such, not every day that you will need to monitor your server, and there are no worries with running it. Also, without impacting the whole Linux OS, you can often restart the separate services because of the way they built Linux. You must rely on a tool called an operating system, going by convention. You can have the game-changing effect of reliability that Linux brings with it if the cost isn't the most significant factor for you. And what is the biggest benefit of the Linux operating system? The biggest reason to adopt Linux is that Linux has overall immunity to random issues of an operating system as well as malicious software and viruses and also its inherent reliability.

Linux saves you money

For you to try out Linux, you won't have to pay anything since Linux has a collaborative and open-source nature. Without licensing payment, it doesn't matter if you have multiple computers; you can go ahead and have the operating system installed freely on them. For many Linux distributions, whether desktop or server editions, this is simply the situation. For example, just for the software installation on one server, concerning the version of 2012, you will have to part with $1,200 to use the Windows Server of Microsoft. You will have additional client access license charges if you are the type that wants several clients to have access to it. And what about the required licenses for you to run web, Windows-based services, etc.? Contrary to that, there is an inclusion of open-source server software in Linux distributions that comes without any cost. Also, without any payment for licensing, you can make use of several web pages. And with just a few clicks, you can have up and running, an entirely efficient Linux web server.

You can easily try Linux

Linux is quite simple to try when you are prepared to experiment with it. If you are feeling hesitant, there's no need for you to have your Windows discarded. You may want to give the preferred operating system a whirl with a live DVD or drive before installing on the hard drive of your PC on a Linux distribution. You will have to install a flash drive or

DVD on a Linux distribution, a bootable system. Then, instead of your drive, have your system configured to boot from that. The fuss and muss are quite minimal as you quickly test-drive some operating systems of Linux, and the primary storage drive you have is safe since it doesn't touch it.

Linux can run on outdated systems

A while ago, they have Windows XP tossed to the wolves, and the Windows Vista is swiftly on the brink to the end. However, some outdated PCs and many people rely on them. If you select a lightweight distribution designed for aging PCs, it can breathe a new life into your computer as well as splashes updated OS on your system. For old PCs, you can choose Lubuntu or Puppy Linux. You will also notice that there is nothing stressful concerning the transition. Since they designed it for Windows XP refugees, there is abundance when it comes to accessing Linux alternatives. For the mimic of feel and look of the operating system of Microsoft, which is highly revered, these distributions provide dedicated "Windows XP Modes."

More sophisticated than before

The desktop's fundamental values are what most main Linux distributors follow. So, the established interface of the PC gets the spit-polish from distributions such as Linux Mint and Fedora, while with the Windows 8 disaster, Microsoft enraged the world. People can wrap their head around some Linux distributions if Windows 7 and Windows XP is their preference. It is typical for them to switch to Linux because of the learning curve that they will need to use Windows 8 or Windows 10. There is also a similarity with the Start menu of the long-established Windows with the Start menu of Linux Mint. Most fundamentally, using it with PC hardware, there is an eradication of the widespread incompatibility of Linux, particularly audio components and networking. Even though with Intel's Secure Boot enabled to have additional steps performed for the installation of Linux on your system, there is a wide range of PC hardware and modern PCs that work with most Linux operating systems. Better yet, to know whether it will work or not before you go ahead with any installation, you can have Linux distributions tested on your system to remember your preference.

There are several compelling reasons you might want to consider to try out Linux on your computer, or at least, give it a hassle-free trial run. And if you are set to go ahead with it, let's discuss the Linux distributions and how you can push forward and make the proper installation of Linux in the next chapter.

Chapter 2: Linux Distributions and Types of Installations

You may have no clear answer if you are asking for the best Linux distributions since, in one way or the other, there are several numbers of Linux distributions, and coming up with an exact amount also can be quite tricky. As some of them appear to be unique, others are simply a clone of one another. Well, that is the beauty of Linux, even if it's a mess. However, you don't have to worry because, below, you will find the list of the best Linux distributions even when there are thousands of them around. Since there is always something for everyone, we must categorize these distributions.

Linux distribution for multi-purpose

For both servers and desktops, as an advanced/beginner-friendly OS, you can utilize some Linux distributions. Thus, you will read below about a separate segment of these distributions, and they are:

Debian:
As an excellent distribution itself, Debian has its base on Ubuntu. Debian tends to be working correctly for not only the desktop but also the servers. Though by scanning through the official documentation, you can quickly get started, it may not be the ideal operating system for beginners. There are some necessary enhancements and several changes introduced by the recent release of Debian 10 Buster. So, test-drive it for you to see!

Manjaro:
The Arch Linux provides the source for Manjaro. For newbies, Manjaro makes it quite easy to use Arch Linux even though it is tailored for advanced users. So have no worries. This Linux distribution is indeed beginner-friendly and straightforward. There are a bunch of useful built-in GUI applications, as well

as a fantastic user interface. While downloading Manjaro, there's an option of selecting a desktop environment. For Manjaro, most people have a preference for the KDE desktop.

Fedora:
The two editions that Fedora provides are separate. It offers for servers and also for laptops/desktops. Those are Fedora Server and Fedora Workstation. Well, Fedora may be your option if you wish to opt for a user-friendly with a possibility of a learning curve for a snappy desktop OS. Anyways, your server can get a fresh breath of a new life when you choose Fedora if you are looking for an operating system for Linux.

Advanced users best Linux distributions

First, before you begin your exploration into Linux distributions that are designed for advanced users only, you need to get comfortable troubleshooting your way to resolve issues with the different package commands and managers. Indeed, there will be a need for you to collect specific requirements if you are a professional. However, it will worth your while to check out these distributions if, as a standard user, you have been using Linux for some time.

Slackware:
Though still delighting in the preference of many people, one of the oldest Linux distributions is Slackware. You may want to consider using Slackware for setting up an ideal environment for yourself if you intend to develop or compile software. Slackware tends to be a fantastic choice for advanced users, even with a significant decrease in the number of developers and users utilizing it. Also, it is believed that Slackware will continue to carry its flagship as one of the best Linux distributions out there with the current news of it getting a Patreon page.

Gentoo:
Gentoo Linux is quite compulsory for anyone who knows how to compile the source code. Though there is a required necessary technical knowledge to make it work, Gentoo is a lightweight distribution. If you need to know some

information about it, you can obtain it through the official handbook. However, to make the most of it might take you a lot of time to figure if you are not sure of what you are doing.

Arch Linux:
This distribution comes with a huge learning curve even though it is a powerful yet simple distribution. Everything you need may not be installed at a time, much unlike others. You will have to add packages required as you configure the system. Also, without GUI, there are a set of commands you will need to follow when you are installing Arch Linux. Also, it may be quite essential to have a clear understanding of some critical things to do after you install Arch Linux if you wish to go ahead with the installation. It's indeed useful to say that there is an active community behind Arch Linux in addition to all the simplicity and versatility. As such, you won't have any need to worry if you run into a problem.

Older computers' best Linux distributions

You can make use of some of the best Linux distributions available if you don't wish to upgrade your system or have an old one lying around. Here are some of the best distributions you can use for your old computers.

Sparky Linux:
For low-end systems, based on Debian, Sparky Linux tends to be a perfect Linux distribution. Different users can enjoy several special editions or varieties provided by Sparky Linux, as well as a fast streaming experience. For example, it rolls releases specific to a group of users while offering a stable version with varieties. For gamers, one familiar type for them is the Sparky Linux GameOver since a bunch of pre-installed games is included in it.

antiX:
As a lightweight Linux distribution and partially responsible for MX Linux, both new and old computers can use antiX. Though working quite correctly, the UI of antiX is not that impressive. Without the need to install it, antiX can be utilized as live CD distribution, and it is based on Debian. For

you not to lose settings with every reboot, you can save the settings as opposed to some other distributions. Not only that, using its feature of "Live persistence," your root directory can also have some changes saved by you. As such, antiX can be your choice if you intend to offer a snappy user experience on old hardware with the use of a live-USB distribution.

Bodhi:
Though it runs well on older configurations, unlike Ubuntu, it is well on top of Ubuntu that they designed and built Bodhi Linux. As a continuation of the Enlightenment 17 desktop, Bodhi Linux's Moksha Desktop is its main highlight. The fast and intuitive streaming is the typical experience users will get for using it. On your older systems, you can as well give it a try even though people's opinion of it is not for personal use.

Solus Budgie:
It is an impressive lightweight desktop OS with Solus 4 Fortitude as a recent major release. Desktop environments such as MATE or GNOME are natural for this when you want to opt into them. However, while being light on system resources, as a beginners' full-fledged Linux distribution, Solus Budgie happens to be one of the favorites of so many people.

Puppy Linux:
One of the smallest distributions you can see out there is Puppy Linux. If you want your outdated system to have a quick system execution, you can give it a try. With the addition of several new useful features, the user experience has improved over the years.

As for some of the lightweight Linux distributions, other options you can try out in this category are Peppermint, Lubuntu, and Linux Lite.

Best distributions of Linux server

Enterprise support, performance, and stability are all that are essential when it comes to a Linux distributions' choice for servers. However, you need to pay attention to some of these recommendations, whether the purpose is for something crucial or a web server when installing it.

CentOS:
For RHEL, you will need to subscribe. Nevertheless, since the sources of Red Hat Linux have been derived from it, RHEL's community edition is quite similar to CentOS. Also, it is a free and open-source as well. For sometimes now, it tends to be an excellent preference. It is considerably less parallel to the number of hosting providers using it. However, people's opinion of CentOS is that of a reliable Linux distribution since its software packages are the latest. On several cloud platforms, CentOS images can be found. You can as well decide on the CentOS image that is self-hosted, which it offers if you don't.

SUSE Linux enterprise server:
There's a need to separate this distribution from OpenSuSE, and as such, there's no need to worry. Maintained by the community, OpenSUSE is an open-source distribution even when everything comes under a standard brand "SUSE." For cloud-based servers, one of the most popular solutions is the SUSE Linux enterprise server. And to manage your open-source solution and to get priority support, you may need to go for a subscription.

Linux Red Hat:
For organizations and businesses, the top-notch platform is the Linux Red Hat. For servers, the highly prevalent range may not be Red hat if we go by the numbers. However, Lenovo, for instance, is among those that have their reliance on RHEL as the primary selection of enterprise users. Technically, there is a correlation between Red Hat and Fedora. And for RHEL to have it on it, anything that Red Hats supports gets tested on Fedora. For you to be sure it will suit your needs, the official documentation of the distribution is worth checking.

Ubuntu servers:

Your server can get unique options depending on where you want it. Ubuntu Cloud may be the perfect ideal for an optimized solution to run Google Cloud Platform, Azure, AWS, and some others. In either case, you can have it installed on your server if you want to opt for Ubuntu Server packages. However, judging by the number, when it comes to deployment on the cloud, the highly popular Linux distribution is Ubuntu. And unless you have particular requirements, the recommendation will be the LTS editions.

As options for a few of the distributions mentioned above, Debian and Fedora are some of the distributions to explore.

Beginners' best Linux distributions

This segment deals with a list of distributions that are quite easy to use. Without the requirement of knowing any tips or commands, you can begin using it right away, and there's no need to dig deeper.

Pop!_OS:

Computer science professionals or developers will experience an excellent pick by Sytem76 from Pop!_OS. If you are beginning to use Linux, it is also quite a great choice as it is not limited to coders. Though the UI feels smooth and a lot more intuitive, it is based on Ubuntu. Also, it enforces full-disk encryption out of the box in addition to the UI.

Zorin OS:

One of the most intuitive and good-looking OS for desktop is another Ubuntu-based distribution, which is Zorin OS. Notably, the recommendation for users without any Linux background will be this distribution after Zorin OS 15 release. It also comes baked in as well as a lot of GUI-based applications. Though ensure to choose the "Lite" edition because you can also install it on older PCs. There are also "Ultimate," "Education," and "Core" editions. However, consider getting the Ultimate version if you intend to help improve Zorin and also support the developers. Otherwise, select the Core edition for free.

MX Linux:

It has been a while now that MX Linux has been in the game. On Distrowatch.com, at present, MX Linux is a highly preferred Linux distribution. You will be amazed as to how you will get familiar with it if you haven't used it before. With Xfce being its desktop environment and also based on Debian, an increasingly popular Linux distribution is MX Linux, unlike Ubuntu. Also, any Mac/Windows user can easily use it as it is packed with several GUI tools in addition to its excellent stability. Also, for installation with one-click facilitation, the package manager is ideally tailored for this. And as one of the sources that are already in the package manager, you will see Flathub there, and in no time, you can install it after searching for Flatpak packages.

elementary OS:

An elegant Linux distribution out there is the elementary OS. It is easy to get comfortable with it if you have already used a Mac-powered system because the UI has a similar resemblance to MacOS. While keeping the performance in mind and also looking as pretty as possible, delivering a user-friendly Linux environment is the focus of this distribution that is based on Ubuntu.

Linux Mint:

Among beginners, another popular Linux is Linux Mint Cinnamon. When Windows XP was discontinued, as a result, many users opted for it since there's a resemblance between Windows XP and the default Cinnamon desktop. It has the applications available for Ubuntu since it is on Ubuntu that Linux Mint is grounded. It becomes a prominent choice for new users of Linux because of the ease of use and simplicity.

Ubuntu:

One of the most undoubtedly popular Linux distributions is Ubuntu, and on several laptops available, you can even find it pre-installed. You will get comfortable with its user interface. As per your requirements, you can easily customize the look of it if you play around. Mainly, theme installation is also another option for you. When you want to get started with

Ubuntu, you will need to learn more about it. Also, Ubuntu users have a massive community that you can find in addition to what it provides. So, go to a subreddit or the forum if you face any issue. You need to check out some coverage online on Ubuntu in case they require direct solutions in no time.

Ultimately, you can give some of these distributions recommended above a try. And quite honestly, the choices will be subjective depending on personal preferences to each of them even when there are quite several Linux distributions that deserve mention.

Server Roles and Types of Installations

Since more operating systems have a great connection with it, this attribute is a unique feature of Linux. Thus, you can have other OS running alongside Linux. With more operating systems in place and for the installation of Linux, the general process of installation is to install Linux again. When you do that, the computer will have 100 percent resources dedication to run Linux. However, as part of an OS sequence which is obtainable on a computer, it is not quite hard to have Linux installed. Also, as an approach you can use to run or install on a computer any distribution of Linux, you can make use of some of these approaches below;

Linux fresh installation
One popular method of installation available is this method. From a DVD/CD, you will install Linux after formatting the hard drive of your computer when you jump into this technique. Then, it is only on the operating system of your computer that Linux will then run. Available methods of installation are:

- PXE

- Kickstart

- Network installation through HTTP, FTP, or NFS

- Hard drive

- CD-ROM

Linux as a VM inside another operating system

Inside another operating system, you may want to consider running Linux as a VM if you prefer to run your favorite open-source software or want an easy way to access a Linux desktop even when you like your current, non-Linux desktop OS. You will need to download and install a Virtual Server application as a simple step, although there are several ways to go by it. Then, under the host software, install your Linux distribution. Thus, you may perform on Linux everything you can do with your other operating system. Even when your other operating systems don't offer some things, there are a lot of things that Linux can provide you.

Live DVD/CD booting Linux

You may choose to try Linux from a Live DVD/CD when you want to retain your primary operating system and to see if you like it, you want to give Linux a try. As a Live CD, several Linux installations offer this running or downloading. As such, from the DVD/CD, Linux will run as an entire operating system that is quite bootable. And instead of running it on a hard drive, you can load your files into the memory of your computer. That means, from a DVD/CD, Linux can be run and then exclusive of any variance, return to its old OS of your system as you remove the DVD/CD when you reboot your computer. Until you discover your preferred choice, you can easily sample some Linux distributions.

Dual-booting

You will have a dual booting system when you want to install Linux and also keep an existing operating system as well. You will then need to decide which one you would like to boot into during the boot process since you will have a PC that can use two different operating systems.

By now, you must be having a bit of understanding of Linux, as well as some distributions that you can use them. Now, it is time to take things further and introduce to you Linux Kernel as well as the operating systems.

Chapter 3: Introduction to Linux Kernel and Operating System

By what means does a computer manage the most complex tasks with such accuracy and efficiency? Well, the short and simple answer is that a computer does everything with the help of the operating system. The operating system makes life easier and performs different tasks through the efficient use of hardware resources. At a high level, there are two parts we can divide the OS. The first part will be the utility programs, while the other is the kernel. The kernel services some of the system resources requests like network connectivity, memory, storage, CPU, and so on, as asked by the various user space processes. And in Linux/GNU, there will be an exploration of the loadable kernel modules by this column. Since the whole operating system solely run in supervisor mode, this makes Linux kernel monolithic. With each subsystem responsible for performing specific tasks, it consists of several subsystems, even though the kernel is a single process. Broadly, these following tasks are performed by any kernel.

Dynamically loadable kernel modules

To ensure that our system is up-to-date, most times, we install security patches and kernel updates. A reboot is often necessary in the case of MS Windows. However, this is far from being suitable. For example, when it is in a production server, the machine cannot be rebooted. Then, without a system reboot, wouldn't it be ideal for removing or adding functionality from or to the kernel on-the-fly? For the kernel modules, the Linux kernels work on the dynamic unloading and loading. And at runtime, any code piece is a kernel module that you can add to the kernel. Without any interruption, when the system is up and running, you can unload and load the modules. You can use the `insmod` command to dynamically link a kernel module to the running kernel and also unlink it by using the `rmmod` command, as an object code.

Networking
One of the vital parts of the operating system is the networking because it works with data transfer between hosts and also allows communication. As routing functionality gets enabled by it, it is also through it that network packets get transmitted, identified, and collected.

Device control
There are several devices required for any computer system. However, for the layer to offer functionality, there is a need for a device driver to make the devices usable. Video/audio drivers, Bluetooth drivers, graphics drivers, and so on are some of the types of drivers present.

File system
The file system heavily influences the Linux/GNU system. Nearly everything is a file in Linux/GNU. Also, conventional for the organization of data hierarchically, journaling and compression of data, deletion, and creation of files, and so on are the storage relation requirements controlled by this subsystem. All primary file systems have the support of the Linux kernel, such as MS Windows NTFS.

Memory management
This subsystem handles every related request. The pages are chunks of fixed size as divided from available memory, and on any demand, can be de-allocated or allocated from or to the process. As it creates the illusions of contiguous ample address space to a physical address space, it also maps the process virtual address with the help of the memory management unit, MMU.

Process management
The life-cycle gets this subsystem to handle the process. Through inter-process communication, it allows data sharing

and connection between processes as it also destroys and creates processes. Also, it enables resource sharing and schedules processes with the help of the process scheduler.

Some Useful Utilities

For the provision of useful information about the kernel modules, Linux/GNU offers several user-space utilities. Now, let's dive into them.

dmesg: though it is a different methodology that the kernel uses, it is on the standard output stream that any user-space program displays its output, i.e., */dev/stdout*. For us to manage the contents of the ring buffer, with the use of the dmesg command, the kernel appends its output to the ring buffer.

modinfo: as a command-line argument, the module that passes such process displays the information by this command. For modules, it searches the */lib/modules/<version>* directory if the argument is not on a filename. Also, it is on the field:value format that modinfo shows each attribute of the module.

It is essential to note that the kernel version is *<version>*, and it is through the execution of the *uname -r* command that we can obtain it.

rmmod: when you want to unload modules from the kernel, you can make use of this command. It is only when the current module is not in use that you can unload. Also used to unload modules forcibly, the *-force* or *-f* has the support of *rmmod*. However, the danger in using this option is extreme, and to remove modules, you can still make use of a safer way. As it waits until the module is no longer used, *rmmod* will isolate the module with the option of *--wait* or *-w*.

The System Preparation

Now, it's action time. An environment for development is all we need to create now. We will have a Debian-based Linux/GNU distribution like Ubuntu and CentOS of a PRM-based Linux/GNU distribution installed as the required packages.

CentOS installation

As a root user and by implementing the command below, the first step is to have the compiler for *GCC* installed:

```
[root]# yum -y install GCC
```

Now, the packages to develop the kernel are the next in the installation level:

```
[root]# yum -y install kernel-devel
```

In conclusion, the utility of the make comes next for the installation:

```
[root]# yum -y install make
```

Ubuntu installation

The compiler for *GCC* is the first in the installation line:

```
[mickey] Sudo apt-get install GCC
```

Then, the packages for kernel development come next:

```
[mickey] Sudo apt-get install kernel-package
```

Then, the utility of the make installation:

```
[mickey] Sudo apt-get install make
```

And we have the kernel module

Now, we have prepared our system. Then, we will need to have the initial module of a kernel written. Using the following contents, use *hello.c* to have the file saved when you open your favorite text editor:

```
#include <linux/kernel.h>
#include <linux/module.h>


Int init_module (void)
{
printk(KERN_INFO □Hello, World !!!\n□);


return 0;
}


void cleanup_module(void)
```

```
{

printk(KERN_INFO □Exiting ...\n□);

}



MODULE_LICENSE(□GPL□);

MODULE_AUTHOR(□Narendra Kangralkar.□);

MODULE_DESCRIPTION(□Hello world module.□);
```

At least, there are two functions for any module. The function of cleanup is the first and second initialization. As such, a cleanup utility is `cleanup_module()` while the initialization function is `init_module()`. And once you load the module and before the module is unloaded, there will be a call for the initialization function, and then the call for the function of cleanup. Other macros, as well as `MODULE_LICENSE`, are quite easy to follow. Relatively the same as `printf()`, the user-space is the syntax, which is a `printk()`. However, at a regular productivity stream, it doesn't print messages, unlike `printf()`. Instead, it is the kernel's ring buffer that receives messages that it appends. There is a priority from each declaration of `printk()`. In the example, `KERN_INFO` priority is used. And between the string of format and `KERN_INFO`, you won't see any comma (,) there. Without the presence of unconditional priority, you can make use of `DEFAULT_MESSAGE_LOGLEVEL` priority. As an indication of success, there is the return `0` in `init_module()` final declaration.

`cleanup_module()` and `init_modules()` are the name of the cleanup and initialization functions. However, we can make use of whichever name in place of cleanup and initialization function with `(>= 2.3.13)`, which is the new kernel. For rearward similarity, there is support for these dated names. In place of the register of the cleanup and initialization functions, the macros provided by the kernel are *module_exit* and *module_init*. Now, with the names of the preference we have for cleanup and initialization functions, let's rewrite the same module:

```
#include <linux/kernel.h>

#include <linux/module.h>

Static int_init hello_init(void)

{

printk(KERN_INFO □Hello, World !!!\n□);


return 0;

}

static void_exit hello_exit(void)

{

printk(KERN_INFO □Exiting ...\n□);


return 0;

}


static void_exit hello_exit(void)

{

printk(KERN_INFO □Exiting ...\n□);

}


module_init(hello init);
```

```
module_exit(hello_exit);

MODULE_LICENSE(□GPL□);

MODULE_AUTHOR(□Narendra Kangralkar.□);

MODULE_DESCRIPTION(□Hello world module.□);

MODULE_VERSION(□1.0□);
```

What we have in this place is that the cleanup and initialization functions imply the _exit and _init keywords.

Module loading and compilation

Right now, the procedure for module compilation needs to be understood. We will make use of the build system of the kernel for the compilation of the kernel module. Before you have it saved as Makefile, you may want to have the process of the collection written down as you, once again, open your favorite text editor. Here, you need to pay attention because you must have a similar directory for the modules of kernel Makefile and hello.c.

There is a requirement for the kernel headers for us to have the modules built. From the kernel's source, the kernel build system is incited by the above makefile, and finally, to complete the module, the makefile of the kernel may have our Makefile invoked. You can complete the process as name hello.ko for the kernel module you develop since, to have the module built, all the requirements are now in our possession.

The first compilation of the first module of the kernel is now successful. Now, it is time to examine the way to, inside a kernel, unload and also load this module. You must take note that to unload or load kernel modules; we need to acquire the root user privileges. You will need to have the command insmod executed when you change to the mode of a super-user to load a module as you will see the following:

34

```
[root]# insmod hello.ko
```

And the success job has been done by *insmod*. However, the output is necessary for us to find. It is the ring buffer of the kernel that the output is appended. Well, through the execution of *dmesg* command, we can as well find out:

```
[root]# dmesg

Hello, World !!!
```

Also, we can verify if or not the module is stocked by using the command *lsmod*:

```
[root]# lsmod | grep hello

hello 859 0
```

All that is required of you is to check the output of the *dmesg* command as you have the command *rmmod* executed. As you see below, to unload the module from the kernel. Now, through the function of cleanup, you will see the message from *dmesg*. Some macros within the module give us the module's information. And in such an attractively configured style below, displaying the information is the command *modinfo*.

How to identify the process' PID

For us to identify a Process ID, which is the existing process's PID, we may need to compose one more module of the kernel. In the header, defined as the *<linux/sched.h>*, it is in the structure of the `task_struct` that the related information of the kernel stocks all progression. As an indicator of the existing process, it offers an *existing* variable. You are only required to have the `current->pid` variable value printed to have the current process PID identified. The *(pid.c)*, a complete code of working, will then be given.

In the object file's name, with a slight modification, similar to an original `makefile` is the `Makefile`. With the use of the `dmesg` command, have the output squared after inserting the module and then make the compilation.

Bridging several files with a module
From a single file, the module compilation has been explored. However, dividing the module into multiple files can be quite convenient, and for a single module, we have multiple source files in a large project. For the building of a module that extends over two files, we must understand the process. From the file `hello.c`, we can divide the cleanup and initialization functions to become two individual files such as `cleanup.c` and `startup.c`. The change will be like this for `cleanup.c`. Then, we will have the exciting part concerning the two modules, the `Makefile`. Self-explanatory enough is the `Makefile`. Now, in our proposition: with the use of `cleanup.o` and `startup.o`, develop the final kernel object. It is time for the compilation and testing of the module. When we utilize the command `modinfo`, we may display module information. From each module, author-related information, license, description, and versions are now shown through the command `modinfo`. It is now the time for output verification by unloading and loading the module for `final.ko`.

The best place to learn more about modules is the kernel source code. When you go online, you can download the latest source code. Right now, we will have to go ahead and discuss in detail how you can install Linux on Virtual Machines. Let's go!

Chapter 4: Installing Linux on Virtual Machine

You might not be sure about dual booting even after installing Linux when you try it from a live CD/DVD. It can be quite useful to use a virtual machine, VM, to install your preferred Linux operating system. What this translates into is that the conditions of a hardware environment are the replication of a software environment. With the limit only coming from the components inside it, the base of your physical PC's hardware is the environment. For example, with two cores, it may be impossible to have on a processor, a virtual four-core CPU. However, on a CPU equipped computer, the outcomes can be far superior, while virtualization can be achieved on many systems. As there are several of them in Windows, for the installation of the Linux operating system to be easy, several virtualization tools are quite available. The one among them to produces the significantly accomplished virtual machine applications is VMware. Now, with the use of VMware Workstation Player, it is time to discover the process of Linux installation in Windows.

VMware Workstation Player Installation

In the initial phase, you will need to have the latest version of the VMware Workstation Player tool downloaded by going to the VMware website. With the 64-bit version, it is about 80 MB for the release of 12.5. For home, personal, and non-commercial use as an evaluation version, you can find VMware Workstation Player for free. For non-profit organizations and students, getting value from the free version is all that makes VMware delighted. As for the functionality factor, the standard virtual machine tasks hosts everything included in the VMware Workstation Player. However, for the business of all levels are the extensive selections of virtualization solutions offered by VMware.

Then, it's time for installation after you must have downloaded VMware Workstation Player. An Enhanced Keyboard Driver installation option will be available for you as you get your guide from a standard installation wizard. Also, you will be able to handle the international keyboards provided by this feature. Just in case, you will see that it's worth installing even as you mightn't need it in the first place. When prompted, restart Windows as you proceed via the installation wizard.

Desired Linux operating system selection

For the kind of Linux that you want to give a try, you likely know it. In a VM, while you will find some Linux distributions not especially suitable, others will be. Conventionally, in VMware, for ARM architecture like the Raspberry Pi, running Linux distributions may not be possible. As such, with the x64 and x86, you may not be able to virtualize the ARM. However, it is time to examine QEMU.

Virtual machine configuration

You can as well proceed with the setting of your VM with the download of your Linux operating system. When prompted, input your email address as you begin to launch VMware Workstation Player. Getting the software for free is what this aspect is all about, and the email list of the VMware gets you on board. The primary application of VMware Workstation Player will load when you have completed that level. And to proceed, your virtual machine will require the creation of an account. The ISO, installer disc image file is the default that you will choose. Note that there is an option of installing the OS later by merely having a blank disk to create a virtual system. Then, you will click "Next" after the installation of your preferred operating system. Your chosen guest OS will install automatically as a message about the installation of VMware Easy Install.

Account creation

Your password, username, and the preferred name are all the information you will enter in the next screen and then hit the "next" button when you name your VM. For the operating system that you are installing, what most times follow its name is the default, and also for your VM, you may go ahead and choose a location. Hit the "next" button again, and you will select the disk capacity for your VM. As a series of files or a file for the physical disk of your computer, this is a saved virtual hard disk. Either option is there for you to select. Meanwhile, you can either alter or accept a recommended size used for your virtual HDD. It could be more than striking because increasing tends to be a safer option. Hit the "next" button again, whatever your choice to come to a screen with "ready to create the virtual machine." Hit on the "finish' button, and the VM will start. So far, after creation, run your virtual machine. Soon, you get the suggestion for the tools of VMware for Linux package, which will arrive through an alert. As an approach to the Easy Installation process, this may not be that necessary. But it's fine when you accept this.

Virtual hardware customization
The customize hardware is another option on the screen for "ready to create..." Now, in another way beyond the HDD, you may want to tweak the hardware of the virtual machine. There are so many options you can choose from, including network adaptor configuration, processors, and memory. You may want to check out the screen of Processors. You will come across a reference to a Virtualization engine in the right-hand pane. This process is already in Automatic by default. As such, indeed, for Linux, you may not have to worry about anything. However, you can set this to Intel VT-x or other alternatives if you run into any problems. Then, in the Memory screen, you can deal with specific issues of performance. Here, also, as a recommended maximum and minimum for your virtual machine, you can see the diagram of the suggested size of RAM. Stick to these recommendations as it tends to be ideal. You may likely slow everything from running the VM software to standard system tasks with the impact on your PC performance when you set the Ram too high, and you will still have issues at hand by going too small.

Ultimately, your settings for display will require a bit of your time. Here, you can decide to set up multiple monitors in your virtual machine or utilize the host computer's monitor settings since you will have the ability to toggle 3D acceleration. There will be a display of a recommended amount as with system memory for the guest operating system, and you can also adjust the graphics memory.

Using Linux in VMware Workstation Player after installation

On a physical desktop machine, it is typical of the operating system installed in the virtual machine to boot the ISO. You can go ahead and automate the entire process through the method of Easy Install, and to apply for setting in the guest, the virtual OS, you can use your Windows host OS configuration. It is useful to pay attention here because you can have the overall control over the operating system installation if you chose the option to install the OS later. Then, you can begin to use the guest OS since you will have access to log into the virtual machine when the installation is complete with the use of Easy Install. As simple as that! Subsequently, with the menu where your virtual machine can be opened, you can also launch the VM.

The Importance of Virtual Machine

For Linux, hardware happened to be a significant encounter in 2005. People were having different issues with USB devices, graphics, Bluetooth, and even wireless. And to make things work, you might have to find wrappers and drivers all the time a new invention came people's way. Since the virtual machine appeared not to be the option, and for any user of Linux to identify the solution, they must interact with the 'real' hardware. However, there have been so many changes. On Linux, a handful of hardware works unplanned. There has been a shift in the focus on the distributions' unique features with less essence on the support for hardware. You can write about them on a similar machine if you can easily play with multiple distributions, and you are a virtual machines' heavy user.

Now, for new users of Linux and the ways they can take advantage of them, let's discuss some benefits of virtual machines even though in the enterprise segment, virtual machines are used extensively.

Who needs to use a virtual machine?
Since there is no availability of specific proprietary services and software, some users of Linux have to boot in twofold. And there is only support for Windows concerning tax filling software as well as some related works by the government in many countries. For you to run Windows software, you can easily use a virtual machine instead of working through the pain and complexity of dual booting. Then, it is only on gaming that the virtual machines may not function. Mainly when you are playing resource-hungry games such as Crysis, to have the desired gaming experience, you may need to talk to real RAM, GPU, and CPU. Since between the hardware and the application, you may not like a virtual layer, video, and audio editing may not work either. Virtual machines work great outside of these and even a few other capacities.

Also, by switching to Linux or formatting the operating system they were used to or playing with Linux, for the individuals that attempt to make a change as non-Linux users, a virtual machine may also be useful. When they are ready, they will have the self-assurance to make the shift since virtual machines get these individuals comfortable with Linux. As such, inside your Windows 10 or Mac OS, you can be running Linux. Above all, to switch between distributions without having to reboot on the same hardware, you can run multiple Linux distributions on virtual machines. Instead of entirely dependent on anyone or being vendor-locked, you will need to be versed with several major distributions as a Linux user. And without having to log out to change the environment, on the same system, you may similarly run various desktop backgrounds with the use of virtual machines. You may not know the type of operating system your client or employer would be using. Thus, in any Linux, you will need some knowledge because you certainly don't want to know only one distribution if you're aspiring to become a developer or system admin. And for testing your applications, you will require several distributions if you are a developer.

As you can see now, working with virtual machines has several advantages. Also, operating virtualization has some significant benefits, which is efficiency, apart from multi-booting. Switching between different distributions and having hard drives formatted can be a waste of your time. So, it is as simple as starting the latest application, and without affecting your work, you can begin a new virtual machine for distribution with virtual machines. A virtual machine can be bliss if you are an enthusiast or distribution-hopper. Keep your attention on several other distributions such as Linux Mint, Fedora, Ubuntu, Kubuntu, OpenSUSE, and so many others even if you are an Arch Linux user. As it takes up space and misuse of financial means, having several physical systems can be virtually impossible. It pays to make a good investment in some multicore processor and more RAM, which can run additional virtual systems than buying six physical machines. Now, you won't experience any form of downtime if, on the same machines, you handle nearly a dozen distributions.

The types of virtual machines to use
You have some alternatives, including VirtualBox, Xen, KVM, Qemu, VMware, and so much more. Others have their advantages and also their disadvantages. Though, solutions such as KVM tend to be quite efficient and more powerful even if you have a preference for VirtualBox. As a new user of Linux, you will find the ease of use of the VirtualBox. And without technical know-how that can be quite hard-core, you can access its tons of functionalities and features. Since VirtualBox can be installed on Mac, Windows, and Linux, and the support for cross-platform is its most significant advantage.

Chapter 5: Linux User Management and System Administration

In computing technology, the major strength is Linux. Linux powers several of the cloud-servers, supercomputers, personal computers, mobile phones, and webservers. In addition to using command-line interface tools and Linux tools to take backups, creating, enhancing, and maintaining user reports or accounts, managing the operations of a computer system is the job of a Linux systems administrator. Linux powers most of the computing devices because of its open-source environment, high security, and high stability. It is essential to know and understand the specific qualities of an administrator of a Linux system:

- Handling users, directories, and file

- Basic bash command

- Managing superuser or root

- Files system hierarchy

- Linux file systems

A Linux administrator's duties
For an institute or organization that needs an excellent IT foundation, a reliable criterion is the system administrator. Hence, all-time requirements will be the need for efficient Linux administrators. As there may be additional duties and responsibilities to the role, from each organization, the job profile might change. Here are a few responsibilities of a Linux administrator:

- During an issue with the server, it is the job of the administrator to troubleshoot.

43

- Essential security tools and system installation. To make necessary recommendations after analyzing hardware requirements, the administrator works with the data network engineer and other departments or personnel.

- Ranging from login issues to disaster recovery, Linux administrator detects and solves the service problems.

- For the Linux environments and its users, creating, maintaining, and enhancing the required tools.

- One of the characters of a Linux administrator is to communicate at all times in a professional, cultivated manner with customers, vendors, and staff.

- Apart from offering excellent customer support for ISP, web hosting, and LAN customers about troubleshooting all increased support troubles, Linux administrator also fixes and analyzes all error logs.

- Part of the duties is listing backup, creating new stored procedures, and taking regular backup of data.

- Internet request maintenance, such as PHP, MySQL, Apache, RADIUS, and DNS.

Linux system admin career process

- Learn how to install and use Linux environment

- Have Linux administration certification

- Become an expert in documentation

- Look for help and support by joining community or group of a local Linux users

Necessarily, taking backup and managing the operations, such as examining hardware and software systems, are a few roles of the Linux systems administrator. Also, the admin must be able to describe technical knowledge understanding quite profoundly.

How to Manage Users and Groups as a Linux Administrator

All at the same time, more than one user can make use of Linux since it is a multi-user operating system. And to manage users in a system, Linux offers a beautiful mechanism. Therefore, getting along with the groups and users in a system is the most significant function of a system administrator. And we will use the CentOS Linux distribution to talk about all the commands used below.

Linux user

The unique identification number, UID, is a binary number that uniquely identifies an account of a user of a system. Normal users and super or root user are the two types of users. There will be limited access to files for the regular users while there will be full access to all the data for super or root user. A user account can be modified, deleted, or added by a superuser. It is in the */etc/passwd/* file that the full account information is stored and also on the */etc/shadow/* file that a hash password is stored.

Using a default setting to create a user

At the command prompt, by running the *useradd* command, a user can be added. Use *passwd* utility to set a password after creating the user like this:

```
[root@localhost handy32]# useradd enirban

[root@localhost handy32]# passwd anirban

Changing password for user anirban.

New password:
```

```
Retype new password:

passwd:    all    authentication    tokens    updated
successfully.
```

There will be an automatic setting of the default shell to
/bin/bash, creation of the home directory
(/home/<username>), and the assigning of a UID by the
system. Anytime the system has added to it a new user and
also uses the user name for the group, a user private group is
created by the useradd command. When a user is created,
specify the full name of the user. For the specification of the
full name of the user, use useradd with the option -c as a
system administrator:

```
[root@localhost    handy32]#    useradd    -c    "Anirban
Choudhury" handy32
```

Using UID to create a user
Using the -u option and a custom UID, a user can be created
like this:

```
[root@localhost handy32]# useradd -u 1036 handy32
```

Using the home directory with a non-default to create a user
By doing the below, you can set a home directory with a non-
default:

```
[root@localhost    handy32]#    useradd    -d    /home/test
handy32
```

Having user added to a supplementary group and primary group

Through the specification of the $-G$ and $-g$ option, it is possible to specify a complementary group and the primary one as an administrator.

```
[root@loaclhost    handy32]#    useradd    -g    "head"    -G
"faculty" handy32
```

User lock and unlock

A user account can be locked or unlocked by a superuser. Using the option $-/$, you only have to invoke *passwd* to lock an account.

```
[root@localhost handy32]# passwd -/ handy32

For user handy32, Locking password

passwd: Success
```

To unlock an account, you can use *passwd* and the $-u$ option:

```
[root@localhost handy32]#   passwd -u handy32

For user handy32 to unlock password

passwd: Success
```

Changing username

For username login change, use *usermod* command with the $-/$ option:

```
[root@localhost handy32]# usermod -/ "nishant" handy32
```

User removal
Using the home directory and a user with the combination of the −r option and userdel:

```
[root@loaclhost handy32]# userdel -r handy32
```

Linux Group

A mechanism used for the collection and organization of users is the Linux group. The group ID, GID, is a uniquely associated ID for each group, like the user ID. We have the supplementary and primary groups as the two types of groups. The primary group belongs to each user and of zero or more than zero complementary groups. It is in /etc/group/ that the information of the group is stored and also in the /etc/gshadow file that the respective passwords are stored.

Using the default setting to create a group
As a root user, run the groupadd command with the default settings to add a new group:

```
[root@localhost handy32]# groupadd employee
```

Using the group name, type gpasswd if you want to add a password:

```
[root@localhost handy32]# gpasswd employee

For group employee, changing the password

New Password:

Re-enter new password:
```

Using a specified GID to create a group

With the use of the $-g$ option, execute the *groupadd* command to specify the group's GID explicitly:

```
[root@loaclhost handy32]# groupadd -g 1200 manager
```

Group password removal

Using the proper group name, run *gpasswd* $-r$ to remove a group password:

```
[root@loaclhost handy32]# gpasswd -r employee
```

Changing the name of the group

As a superuser, use the $-n$ option as you run the *groupmod* command to change the name of the group:

```
[root@loacalhost handy32]# groupmod -n hrsupervisor employee
```

Changing the GID of the group

Along with $-g$, run the *groupmod* command to change the group's GID:

```
[root@loaclhost handy32]# groupmod -g 1050 manager
```

Deleting a group

You will first need to delete the users of that primary group before you can delete a primary group. With the group name, run the `groupdel` command to delete a group:

```
[root@loaclhost handy32]# groupdel employee
```

The File System of Linux

The technique of storing files on a hard disk is a file system. And Linux supports several types of file systems including:

- Special-purpose file systems: debugfs, tmpfs, sysfs, procfs, etc.

- Flash storage file systems: YAFFS, JFFS2, ubifs, etc.

- Conventional disk file systems: NTFS, JFS, Btrfs, XFS, ext4, ext3, ext2, etc.

The hierarchy standard of the file system

The file system hierarchy is a standard layout used to store files for the Linux system. Here are some directory structures for the most common Linux:

The online manual page for Linux

There is a help or support for every single command for Linux, and this is one of the key features of Linux. You will have to type the following command for the manual page of the Linux to be accessed:

```
[handy32@localhost~]$man /s
```

The command page of the manual will be provided when you do this.

Root or superuser

For anyone to do any alteration to a service or program of Linux with access to all kinds of permission, this account is a special kind of user account. To become root or superuser, you will use the *su* command and to become one, all you have to do is to enter the root password by typing the following command:

```
[handy32@localhost~]$su
```

Directories and files handling

Everything is a file inside Linux. As such, through file operation related commands, there's an interaction with them during the time of dealing with device files or standard text files. Below are a few operations on the files:

File creation:

For the creation of a file, two commands are quite necessary, and they are *cat* and *touch*. To create an empty file, you can make use of the *touch* by following the example below:

```
[handy32@loaclhost~]$touch file1
```

To view or create a file, you will use the *cat* which you do by following this step:

```
[handy32@loacalhost~]$cat>file1
```

Also, you can use the command below to view a file type:

```
[handy32@localhost~]$cat file1
```

Copying a file:
For you to copy a file from one location to another, you can use the *cp* command like this:

```
[handy32@localhost~]$cp file1 /home/sandra/Documents/
```

The current working directory will be copied by this command to */home/bhargab/Documents/*.

Removing a file:
You can type the command below to remove a file:

```
[handy32@localhost~]$rm file1
```

Moving or renaming a file:
To rename or move a file; the command you can use is the *mv*. Use below command to move a file from one place to another:

```
[handy32@loaclhost~]$mv file /home/sandra/Document
```

Under */home/sandra/*, the Document directory will get the file1 with the use of the above command. Then, from file1 to file2, you can perform the below command to rename a file.

```
[handy32@loaclhost~]$mv file1 file2
```

Directories and files listing:

The contents are the `ls` lists, which are directories and files of the specified directory or current directory. For the contents of the current directory to be displayed, use the below command:

```
[handy32@localhost~]$ls
```

The directory name, as well as the file name, will be listed by this command. You can use the command below to list all files in the hidden files and also your home directory:

```
[handy32@localhost~]$ls □a
```

With the / option, type `ls` to view files in a long-listing format:

```
[handy32@localhost~]$ls □l
```

Below, you will see a portion of the output:

```
Total of 48

drwxr-xr-x. 2 handy32 handy32 4096 Jan 25 21:32
Desktop
drwxr-xr-x. 2 handy32 handy32 4096 Apr 24 16:33
Documents
drwxr-xr-x. 6 handy32 handy32 4096 Jan 20 23:55
Downloads
-rw-rw-r--. 1 handy32 handy32    1024 Apr 28 22:18
file1
-rw-rw-r--. 1 handy32 handy32    1024 Apr 28 22:01
file2
-rw-rw-r--. 1 handy32 handy32    1024 Apr 28 22:01
file3
drwxr-xr-x. 2 handy32 handy32 4096 Dec 20 08:48 Music
drwxr-xr-x. 2 handy32 handy32 4096 Dec 20 08:48
Pictures
drwxr-xr-x. 2 handy32 handy32 4096 Dec 20 08:48
Public
drwxr-xr-x. 2 handy32 handy32 4096 Dec 20 08:48
Videos
```

48 is the total number of disk blocked, as indicated by the total 48. In each of the lines, there are nine columns, and the following permission was represented by each column, including file name, time and date, bytes sizes, group name, and numbers of links. There are 10 subfields in the permission field, and the type of file is what the first field represents. The (u) permission denotes the next three fields, while the representations of the group (g) permissions are the seventh, sixth, and fifth fields. The (o) permissions have its representation in the last three fields with read permission from (r), execute permission from (x), and write permission from (w).

The soft and hard links
In the hard disk, a connection between the actual data and a file name is a link, and these, are soft and hard links. When you follow the command below, you can create a hard link:

```
[handy32@loaclhost~]$ln file1 file2
```

54

And by following the command below, create a soft link:

```
[handy32@localhost~]$ln □S file1 file3
```

Changing Mod:

For every file in Linux, there are three types of connected permission, and they are (x) for execute, (w) for write, and (r) for read. Through the superuser or the owner of the file, it is easy to change the existing file permission. To embed a *write* permission to the group, use the command below:

```
[handy32@localhost~]$chmod g+w file1
```

Also, use the following command for other users to have an execute permission:

```
[handy32@localhost~]$chmod o+x file1
```

You may use the following the command below when you want to take away execute permission from a group:

```
[handy32@localhost~]$chmod g-x file1
```

Current working directory

Below, you will see the display of the current working directory through the *pwd* command:

```
[sandrahandy32@localhost~]$pwd

/home/sandra
```

As such, the */home/sandra/* is the current working directory.

Directory creation:
For the creation of a directory, you can use the *mkdir* command like this:

```
[sandrahandy32@localhost~]$mkdir myDir
```

Under */home/sandra/*, a directory will be created.

Directory removal:
For an empty directory to be removed, you will use the *rmdir* command like this:

```
[sandrahandy32@localhost~]$rmdir MyDir
```

You will also remove the parent directories and not only the specified directory with the *p* option using *rmdir*.

```
[handy32@localhost~]$rmdir □ p myDir.
```

So far, we have covered extensively so many angles on the system administration and also Linux user management.

You may want to go back and read through them for some time to get abreast of some of the things discussed in this segment. When you do, you can get over to the next section, where we will go in-depth on Linux directory structures.

Chapter 6: Linux Directory Structures

There are needs for data storage on an HDD, hard disk of several types, or a few similarities, including a USB for every general-purpose computer. These needs come with a couple of reasons. In the first place, anytime you switch off your computer, the contents of the RAM can be lost. And as for the use of solid-state drives and USB memory sticks, after the removal of power, the maintenance of the stored data in them tends to be the function of non-volatile RAM types. Quite expensive is the flash RAM than other related categories like the volatile, standard RAM such as DDR3. The disk space is not as expensive as the standard RAM because the data storage by hard drives tends to be the second reason. Regarding per byte cost, RAM is still more useful. There's been a rapid drop in the value of both disk and RAM. As per unit, the hard drive is about 71 times less expensive the RAM, based on a 2TB hard drive costs against 16GB of RAM as a quick calculation of the cost per byte.

In a few confusing and different ways, there are a lot of discussions from several quarters about filesystems. With regards to the perspective of a document or analysis, you will need to distinguish the exact meaning since the word itself can have multiple meanings. For using it in distinctive conditions and based on people's observations, let's attempt to define several meanings of the term 'filesystem.' The intention is to make this definition grounded on its several handlings as we strive to adapt to the conventional official meanings.

1. With a specific kind of filesystem, a formatted logical or partition volume that, on a Linux filesystem, can be mounted on a specified point.

2. A particular formatted data storage like XFS, BTRFS, EXT4, EXT#, EXT2, etc. 100 filesystems types have support on Linux, including the newest in addition to the oldest. And to define accessing and storing the data, these filesystem varieties function by its metadata structures.

3. The start of the entire Linux directory structure is at the top (/) root directory.

Basic functions of the filesystem

There are specific inescapable and exciting details that the disk storage encompasses with it as a necessity. Essentially, the provision of non-volatile data storage is one of the ultimate functions and purposes of a filesystem. However, from that requirement, there are some other essential functions. The provision of a namespace is what the whole filesystems have to execute; a methodology of organizational and naming. And out of the entire set of characters available, this process defines the manner with which you can brand a file, particularly the subset of characters and the length of a filename that you can use in place of filenames. Also, atop a disk, the data's logical structure is what it defines, including limping files in a vast, single conglomeration as well as for organizing files with the directories usage. For the provision of that namespace's rational base, quite necessary is the structure of metadata when the namespace has been defined. As such, for the support of a classified directory structure, there is an obligatory addition of data structures. These structures make the determination of the used space blocks upon the disk as well as those available. As for the maintenance of the directories' names and files, the structures that allow that and also the statistics about the data position or locations which, on the disk, belong to the folder, last accessed or modified, as well as times and sizes they were created. For the storing of the sophisticated material of the disk's subdivisions, they make use of other metadata, including logical partitions and volumes. It represents the structures and more complex metadata, which, separated and independent of the filesystem metadata, confine the data expressing the filesystem accumulated on the partition or drive.

Also, for the provision of access to the function of the system calls that control filesystem objects such as directories and files, API, Application Programming Interface is also required for filesystems. The tasks of deleting, moving, and creating files are provided by the APIs. Including the location on a filesystem that you place a file, part of the things APIs offer is algorithms that determine things. For minimizing and speeding the disk fragmentation, objectives may be the purpose of such algorithms. As a pattern for rights of entry definition to directories and files, there is also a security model in the place provided by modern filesystems. As a user, you can have a way into other people's files or the OS as a result of the Linux filesystem security model. For the implementation of these purposes, the required software is the ultimate building block. And as a technique to enhance programmer efficiency and both system, the application of two-part software is what Linux uses. The virtual filesystem of Linux is this implementation's first part of the two. For the access to the filesystems of all types and also the provision of a single command set for the developers and the kernel is done by this virtual filesystem. And the driver of the specific required device to interface gets a call from the virtual filesystem software to the several kinds of filesystems. The second section of the execution is the drivers of the filesystem-exclusive appliance. On the logical or partition volume and to those explicit to the types of the filesystem, the filesystem commands' standard set is interpreted by the device driver.

Directory Structure of Linux

The file system structure of Linux can appear particularly alien if you are the type that is coming from Windows. Now mostly with three-letter names, the cryptic-sounding directories and a / option have replaced the forgotten drive letters as well as the $C:\backslash$ drive. What defines some other Unix-related OS and the structure of file systems on Linux is the FHS, Filesystem Hierarchy Standard. However, also contained in the Linux filesystems are some directories that are not yet defined by the standard.

/var – Variable Data Files
As it must be read-only in the usual operation, the writable counterpart to the /usr directory is the /var directory. During normal operation, we can write to the /var directory the log files as well as all things else that would normally be written to /usr. For example, in /var/log, the log file can be found there.

/usr – Read-Only Data & User Binaries
Contrary to files and applications that the system uses, users use files and applications that contain the directory /usr. For example, rather than the directory /sbin, the location of the non-elemental binaries of the system administration, the location of non-essential applications is within the directory /usr/bin. There are other directories contained in the /usr directory, including architecture-free folder such as graphics which share location in /usr/. This process prevents them from mucking up the rest of the system, where the local directory usr/ is, by default, found installed in the locally assembled applications.

/tmp – Temporary Files
Whenever your system is restarted, since it is in the /tmp directory where application stored temporary files, the utilities like tmpwatch will have these files deleted at any time.

/srv – Service data
The 'data for services provided by the system' is contained by the /srv directory. You would probably store the files of your website in a directory inside the /srv directory if you were using the Apache HTTP server to serve a website.

/selinux SELinux Virtual File System

With SELinux, the directory /selinux contains special files if, for security purposes, Red Hat and Fedora use SELinux by your Linux distribution. It is the same as the /proc. On Ubuntu, this folder's presence appears to be a bug since Ubuntu doesn't use SELinux.

/sbin – System Administration Binaries
The directory /bin is parallel to the directory /sbin. And for system administration, it is generally intended to be run by the root user as it contains essential binaries.

/run – State Files Application
For the requirement, such as process IDs and sockets, to store transient place, the directory /run gives a standard place application as it is fairly new. Since files in /tmp may be deleted, /tmp can't store these files.

/root – Home Directory for Root
The home directory for the root operator is the directory /root. As the system root directory, its location is at /root instead of /home/root for the location.

/proc – Kernel & Process Files
Since it doesn't contain standard files, the directory /dev is the same as the /proc directory. Special files to process and represent information are all that it contains.

/opt – Optional Packages
For optional software packages, these directories are contained in the directory /opt. Since the standard filesystem hierarchy doesn't have its respect, the proprietary software commonly uses it. For instance, as you install it, it might dump the files of proprietary programs in /opt/application.

/mnt – Transitory Mount Points
While using them, where the temporary filesystems are mounted by the system administrator is the directory /mnt. For example, for the execution of a few operations of file recovery, you may well want to mount a partition on windows /mnt/ for Windows if you are mounting it.

However, to mount other system files, you may choose any space on the system.

/media – Removable Media

Where the devices inserted into the computer are mounted is where subdirectories contain the /media directory. For instance, a directory will automatically be created inside the /media directory as you insert a CD into your Linux system. And inside this directory, you can access the contents of the CD.

/lost+found – Recovered Files

There is a `lost+found` directory in each filesystem of Linux. As such, a filesystem check will be performed at the next boot if the filesystem crashes. And for the extensive recovery of data, it is in the `lost+found` directory will any corrupted files found be placed.

/lib – Essential Shared Libraries

In the /sbin and /bin directories, required essential binaries are contained libraries in the /lib directory. Binaries needed by libraries within a /usr/bin folder are located within /usr/lib.

/home – Home Files

For each user, the directory /home contains a file for home. For example, /home/greg will be the location for the home folder if your username is Greg. User-explicit formation file and user's data files are contained in this home folder. On the system, for you to have other files modified as the superuser, each user needs to obtain elevated permission even when they only have the write access to their home folder.

/etc. – Configuration Files

Though easily edited by hand in a text editor, the maintenance of the configuration files is contained by the /etc. directory. Be aware that the system-wide configuration files are contained by the /etc/ directory, and it is in each home directory of the user that user-specific configuration files are located.

/dev – Devices Files

As files, devices are exposed by Linux. As such, devices that have the representation of some special files are the directory /dev. Though they seem like files, much known to us, we can't call them original files. For instance, in the system, the major SATA drive is represented by the /dev/sda. For you to inform it to edit /dev/sda, you could begin a compartment editor if you want to partition it as virtual devices without any hardware correlation. Also, pseudo-devices are contained in this directory. For example, there are only random numbers that the /dev/random produces. As it creates no output, an exceptional device is /dev/null that instinctively have all inputs discarded when, toward /dev/ null, a command's output is piped.

/cdrom – CD-ROMs Historical Mount Point

A directory that doesn't belong to the standard of FHS is the directory /cdrom. However, when you go to Ubuntu and other OS, you will find it. For CD-ROMs inserted in the system, it is a temporary location. However, it is inside the /media directory for the standard location of temporary media.

/boot – Static Boot Files

The files needed to boot the system is contained by the /boot directory. For example, stored here are your Linux kernels and the GRUB boot loader's files. Though their location with other files is in the /etc directory, the configuration files of the boot loader are not located here.

/bin – Essential User Binaries

When the system is mounted in a single-user mode, the essential user binaries, otherwise known as programs that must be present, are contained within the /bin directory. It is in /usr/bin that applications like Firefox is stored, while the location for vital utilities and system programs like bash shell are in /bin directory. You can also store in another partition the /usr directory. Though, even if no other filesystems are mounted, you will be sure to have these essential utilities when you place these files in the /bin directory. As it contains crucial binaries for system administration, similar to it is the /sbin directory.

/ - the Root Directory

Known as the root directory, it is under the / directory that you can locate everything on the Linux system. On Windows, the C:\ directory is quite similar to / directory. However, since Linux doesn't have drive letters, this is not strictly true. On Windows, while D:\ is the location for another partition, on Linux, it is in another folder under / directory that other partition would appear.

Chapter 7: Working with Disk, Media, and Data Files (gzip – tar)

Before you can use them, you must structure storage devices like USB drives and hard drives since the regular practice in Linux is deleting and creating partitions. *Partitions* often host separate sections of devices with considerable storage after they have been divided. Also, you can divide into isolated parts of the hard drive using the partitions where, as a discrete hard drive, each section behaves as such. If you administer several OS, partitioning can be particularly useful. In Linux, otherwise known as disk partition manipulation, you can remove or create this with the use of several powerful tools. As such, devices with large disk can benefit as well as several disk partitions, and we will go in-depth on how to use the `parted` command. Here are some common commands like `cfdisk` and `fdisk`, as well as the difference between `parted`.

- **Reliability**: in a DOS partition, only one copy of the partition table is stored. At the end and the beginning of the disk, two copies of the partition table are kept by the GPT. Also, done with DOS partitions to check the partition table integrity, the GPT uses a CRC checksum.

- **More partitions**: it is only 16 partitions that the tables of DOS partition permit with the use of extended and primary partitions. Having many more is what you can choose and by default, can get up to 128 partitions with GPT.

- **Larger disks**: in some cases, up to 16TB is possible even though a partition of the DOS table tends to format up to 2TB of disk space. However, up to 8ZiB of space can be addressed by a GPT partition table.

- **GPT format**: while, to DOS partition tables, `cfdisk` and `fdisk` are limited, a Globally Unique Identifiers Partition Table, GPT can be created by the `parted` command.

It is recommended to use `parted` to function with disk partitions because working with them will require more flexibility in today's larger disks. Most often, part of the operating system installation process is the creation of the disk partition. When an existing system is getting an addition of a storage device, direct use of the `parted` command is most useful.

Analyze Disk Space and Hard Disk Partition on Linux with These Commands

For you to check the partitions on your systems, there are some commands you can use. Part of what the commands might do is checking what partitions exist on every floppy disk and some additional details such as filesystem, consumed space, total size, so many others. Though they can also modify them, there are some tools for partitioning where the partition material can be displayed, including `cfdisk`, `sfdisk`, and `fdisk`.

hwinfo
You can make use of `hwinfo` to print out the partition and disk list, as a general-purpose hardware information tool. However, like the other commands, the output doesn't print details about each partition.

blkid
Though it doesn't report the space on the partitions, `blkid` prints the block devices, storage and partitions media, attributes such as `uuid` and file system type.

lsblk
Optical drives and disk partitions, as well as all the storage blocks, are listed out by `lsblk`. If any, it lists out the mount point and, most notably, the total size of the block/partition.

On the partitions, free/used space is not reported. It indicates that the filesystem is not yet mounted if there is no MOUNTPOINT. Also, it means that there is no disk for DVD/CD. With a device such as the model and label, `lsblk` is capable of displaying more information.

pydf
Written in Python is the improved version of `pydf`, and in an easy to read manner, it prints out all the hard disk partitions. Also, it is only the mounted file systems that `pydf` is limited to show.

df
This command prints out details about only mounted filesystems even though it is not a partitioning utility. Even filesystems that are not real disk partitions are some of the list generated by `df`. When you use it, you will discover that the actual partitions or devices are only the file systems that start with a `/dev`, and to filter out the real hard disk partitions or filesystems, you can use `grep`. Then, use `df` to display only actual disk partitions with the type of partition.

parted
If needed, this modifies the list as it also lists out the partitions being another command-line utility.

cfdisk
Based on `ncurses` with an interactive user interface, the partition editor of Linux is `cfdisk`. Use it to modify or create current partitions in addition to listing out those partitions. One partition can only run at a time with `cfdisk`, and as such, pass the device name to `cfdisk` if the details of a specific disk are required.

sfdisk
In addition to a goal similar to `fdisk`, however, with additional features, another utility is `sfdisk`. Each partition's size can be displayed in MB.

fdisk

For the checking of the partition on a disk, the most commonly used command is the `fdisk`. Like filesystem type, you can get the display of the partitions and details with the use of the `fdisk` command. However, each partition size report may not be available with `fdisk`.

Linux Data Manipulation

It can be confusing with the Linux world if you are the type that is quite used to Windows. What with no image, link, or anything to click, few hints, no wizards, and so on. And also, before anything can be done, you need to know what it is you want. Let's assume that, somehow contrary to your interest, you have no choice but to use the shell prompt of Linux and learning the agonizing, cryptic program where the xkcd forms its basis does not tally with your burning desire. However, for the processing of your data, the use of the command-line might have in it some good reasons. Attempting to make use of Excel to deal with this data may not be suitable even with the new technologies offering digital data terabytes and more instruments providing a digital output. You may not also get anywhere near luck with the use of CSV files. However, with the use of free, reasonably simple utilities on Linux, these can be easily managed. Also, another reason for taking this path is that the powerful mainstream tools for Linux come with no cost.

Though we may want to leave out most of these, however, SAS, Mathematica, MATLAB, and so on have been ported to Linux and are a few excellent branded tools. As it works better on Linux and as second nature on Linux, we may not imply that using native applications and utilities may not do well on Windows. Also, there is a constant assurance that on Linux, it will work always. Since there's a payment option for Apple and Microsoft in money and time by releasing yet another pointless upgrade to bump their profit, you don't need to learn a new interface every 6 months.

Identifying the file type

It is possible you are not aware of the kind of data it is even though the data might have been generated in the lab. The file is a device that can proffer some help even though it is not foolproof. The response it tends to give comes from the question: "what file type is it?" If there are any diagnostic characteristics, file peeks inside the file to see them, unlike the endings of the file name mapping approach of Windows, which has filename.typ to a specific type. And it can be quite helpful suppose there's been name-mangled or renamed in translation to the file.

Hypotheses

With the installation of Linux standard famous utilities, including R, the hypothesis is that on a Linux, you have access to a bash shell. For this exercise, a directory can be created. For DataDir, it is quite on $DDIR that you can give it your reference, though you can give it any name you like. And to the DDIR variable of the shell, you may as well have actual term assigned to it:

```
Export DDIR=/stephen/leo/
```

bash> is the prefix of the shell commands and to test your shell, including comments with embed (with # as a prefix; you may as well ignore them) can mouse into it. Also, you may want to ignore the prefix bash>. Also, at the UC Irvine and on the cluster nodes of the interactive BDUC, accessible here are all the defined utilities. And for any Linux distribution, you can get them without any costs, except they state otherwise.

The size of the file

red+blue all.txt.gz, a tab-bordered data file of 25MB is what we are going to use. By pressing upon the link with a right-clicking, you can download it in Firefox and hit 'save.' For this exercise, use the directory $DDIR to save it. Then, use *gunzip blue+red_all.txt.gz* to decompress it. After that, with *ls*, the result of the entire bytes will be achieved.

Using Linux to Mount and Unmount Media
With the use of the operating system of a Linux, you can have media mounted and unmounted with this process. You must be aware that the default Red Hat installation is what this process uses, and thus, with the use of other Linux operating system types, the commands, structures, and file names might not be the same. Now, let's get down to the business!

If you are mounting a CD, follow the steps below:

1. Ensure that, on your server, there is a presence of the */nt/cdrom* directory. You can type *mkdir/mnt/cdrom* if there's no existence of this directory. Then, hit the 'enter' button.

2. Then, have *mount/dev/scd0 -t iso9660 -o ro /mnt/cdrom* typed for you to mount the CD. Again, hit the 'enter' button.

If the disk is the instrument you want to mount, you can follow the below command:

1. Be certain that on the server, you have */mnt/floppy* directory. You may want to type the below command if there's no existence of this directory:

   mkdir/mnt/disk

Again, hit the 'enter' button.

2. You can type the following command to have the disk mounted:

   mount/dev/sda -o auto/mnt/disk

Then, hit the 'enter' button.

For you to unmount the media, you can follow the command below:

1. Input CD and hit enter.

2. Follow the commands below:

- You can type the command below if it is your CD that you want to unmount:

  unmounts /mnt/cdrom

Then, hit the 'enter' button.

- You can type the command below if it is a disk that you want to unmounts:

  unmounts mnt/floppy

Again, hit the 'enter' button.

Creating from the Command-line a File for Tar GZip

If you are managing your backups away from Time Machine or you want to have file groups transferred, having the zip files made could have been something you are probably doing. The command line can be an excellent option for you to make a gzip and tar archive if you prefer better compression and also additional advanced options using the user-friendly and accessible tools of GUI zip. And typical of Linux elements, even in Mac OS X, the syntax will be similar.

Bundle creation the archive of tar gzip

You can make use of the syntax from the (terminal/applications/) command-line. For example, you could have jpg files directories compressed by typing some specific commands.

Here, a wildcard is the *, which means that you can have .jpe compressed from any file that has the extension .jpg, and that is all. Though offering compression on its own, tar packages become a bundle of a single file from a set of files as two distinctive products are the resulting `.tar.gz.` file. Therefore, gzip compression is quite valuable to supplement for you to have the tar compressed. And if you want it, you can have them as different commands while running them. However, as you can automatically have the tar file gzipped since the flag `-z` is what tar command offers, there is no much need for it.

Chapter 8: File, Directory Manager, Permissions, Networking, and SSH

As a layer generally, the operating system that handles your data positioning on the storage is any filesystem on Linux. And even if you discover any unsupported filesystem type, you will not know which file starts where and what files end where without it. For software that can deal with it, you may even download it. As such, what are the Linux filesystem types? You will notice that Linux provides several filesystems such as the ones below when you attempt to install it: swap, btrfs, jfs, ext4, ext3, ext2, ext

Therefore, what are these filesystems that Linux provides?

Btrfs
Oracle made this one, and in some distributions, it is not entirely stable as Ext. However, if you have to, you may think that it is a replacement for it, and it has excellent performance.

XFS
Using it with small files, it works slowly being an old filesystem

JFS
IBM made this old filesystem and, whether, with big or small files, it works quite well. However, after a long time, as indicated by reports, it failed, and files get corrupted.

Ext4
With a significant speed, this gives room for large files. If you are looking for an option for SSD disk, you may want to go for this, and it is the suggested default filesystem you will see when you want to install Linux.

Ext3

With backward compatibility and upgrades, it comes with Ext2. And since this filesystem doesn't give any support for disk snapshots or file recovery, servers no longer use this type of filesystem.

Ext2
This gives room for 2 terabytes of data allowed as the Linux first filesystem.

Ext
Because of limitations, people are no longer using this old one.

High-Level Explanation
Now is the time to know from the high-level, what is inside those filesystems since you are familiar with the Linux filesystem. If you are someone coming from Windows, it will be possible to install partitions such as D:\ and C:\, usually C:\, because Windows has partitions like them. Though we have discussed it in some previous chapter, what is the filesystem structure of Linux? You will see the Linux filesystem hierarchy when you navigate to the root partition, which is /.

Linux Directory Management Commands
For us to translate between IP addresses and domain names, the domain name system, DNS, is what we utilize. For example, on a Linux system, for DNS hookup, you may use the host command or dig command. Similarly, it is not by inode number but by file names that people refer to Linux files. As such, what is the directory's actual function? It is according to your usage that you tend to group the files. For example, you can do that under /etc/ directory that all configuration files are stored. Thus, making a connection between the file names and their connected inode number is the purpose of a directory. And you will discover two sub-directories inside every directory named:

1. .. (double period) – the pointer to the previous directory, i.e., the directory above the one you are in at

present. Except for the root directory, it is in every directory that the ".." appears. And to the same inode as ". " that the ".." always points.

2. . (single period) – which means the current directory

For us to list directories and files, we can use the `ls` command, including on Linux .. and . directories.

```
ls -la
```

Directory

A sub-directory is contained inside another directory. A tree structure forms at the end of the directories and to see directory tree structure, use the tree command:

```
$ tree /etc | less
```

Typical of a file, a directory has an inode. As it connects each name with an inode number, it is a specially formatted file containing records. Under ex2/3 filesystem, it is quite vital to take note of the following limitation of directories:

- There is a chance for an unlimited number of subdirectories in Ext4 and other modern Linux filesystems

- In a single directory, there is a soft upper limit of about 10-15k files

- In a single directory, there is an upper limit of 32768 subdirectories

However, without any issues, using a hashed directory index, which is under-development, allows 100k-1M+ files in a single directory, according to the official documentation of ext2/3 filesystems. And related to directory, below are some bash shell alias commands:

```
alias ..='cd..'

alias d='ls -l | grep -E "^d"'
```

Linux directory management commands
For you to work with files and directories, here is a list of standard Linux commands:

Command	Description	Example(s)
diff command	Compares the content of any two files	`diff old.c new.c`
egrep command	Though, extended regular expression supported, it is the same as grep	`egrep -I 'err|cri|warn|' /var/log/messages`
grep command	In the specific files, it finds a specific search string	`grep "nameserver" /etc/resolv.conf`
more command	At a time, through text one screenful, it serves as a filter for paging.	`more /etc/hosts`

less command	The content of the specified file is seen by it.	*less resume.txt*
cat command	Displays the contents of a file	*cat data.txt*
file command	This detects the contents of the specified files.	*file /etc/resolv.conf*
find command	In a given directory, this searches for a file	*find $HOME -name "hello.c"*
locate command	Finding in which directory of a specified file is located	*locate file!*
chmod command	Changes the access permissions	*chmod 0444 dir1*
chgrp command	With the specified group name, this command transfers the group ownership of a given file to the group.	*chgrp dir1*
chown command	With the specified username, it transfers ownership of a file.	*chown username file*

In command	From source to target, it creates an internal link	`ln -s /etc/hosts/tmp/link`
rm command	From the filesystem, this command removes the specified files, and unless the option -r is used, `rm` doesn't remove directories	`rm files!` `rm -r dir1`
cp command	Copies source to the target	`cp -r dir1 /path/to/dir2`
mv command	Deleting the source after copying to the target	`mv dir1 dir2`
cd command	cd changes to the home directory of the user without any parameters	`cd`
pwd command	This command displays the name of the working or current directory.	`pwd`
cd .. command	Go back to the previous directory.	`cd ..`
cd command	Change the current directory	`cd /etc/`
	If it is already empty, this deletes the	

rmdir command	specified directory.	*rmdir dir1*
mkdir command	A new directory is created through this command.	*mkdir dir1*

Managing Directories

Since, from Nautilus, you can copy, move, delete, or create them, you must learn to treat your directories like files and related to files directories with the use of commands from a shell prompt.

Creating directories

For you to have a fresh sub-directory conceived, you must learn to write permission. It is at the /temp/ directory and the home directory, as well as the subdirectories that most users have these permissions. You will have to navigate to your new directory for you to use Nautilus in creating an original directory. In the window's blank potion, right-click and then choose to create a folder. Then, using the untitled folder with the highlighted text, a new folder icon will appear. Before you hit the 'enter' button, remember to give this new folder a name. When you attempt to use a shell prompt to have an original directory conceived, the `mkdir` command is all you need to use. You can replace the `<directory-name>` by simply type in: `mkdir <directory-name>` with the new directory's intended title.

Deleting directories

It is on the Desktop that you click and then **Trash** the icon or move it to the Trash after right-clicking on it to delete a directory from Nautilus. You will need to enter the `rmdir` command to delete a directory that is empty from the prompt of the shell. It is the `rm -rf <directory>` command that you

80

will need for you to delete an unlikely empty directory and also all the things within such directory.

Dot directories

Dotfiles are also part of the applications created by "dot" directories. Also, other files required by the application, a hidden directory of configuration, is a directory for dot, and these files are a single hidden configuration file. Generally, these directories are user-specific non-configuration files, and their accessibility is to the user that has them installed.

Linux File Permissions

Since several users can have access simultaneously, and as a multi-user operating system, Linux is a clone of UNIX. Also, without any modifications, anyone can use Linux in servers and mainframes. However, because vital data can be removed, changed, or corrupted by malign or unsolicited individuals, this situation raises security concerns. As such, there are two levels of authorizations divided by Linux for adequate security, and they are:

1. Permission

2. Ownership

In Linux, a critical concept is ownership and permissions. We will begin the discussion with the Ownership as both of them will be examined.

Linux file ownership

There are 3 types of owners assigned for every directory and file on your Linux system.

Group:

There are multiple users contained in a user-group. Also, similar access permissions to the files will be given to all users belonging to a group. Several individuals will require access to a file if you have a project. You can go ahead and add all users to a group instead of manually assigning permissions to each user. Then, no one else can modify or read the files when you assign group permission to file.

User:
The owner of the file us a user, and you will be the owner if, by default, you are the one who creates a file. Thus, as an owner, you can also be called a user.

Other:
This case points to having access to a file by any other users. This type of user does not belong to a user group that owns the file or created the file. Mostly, this can be anyone else. Therefore, it is also referred to as setting permissions for the world when you set permission for others.

Ultimately, the question of distinction arises. How can you go about separating these three user types without exposing vital information from one group to another group? It is typical of hidden your image from your computer from your colleague who works on your Linux computer. Now, this is the case of permissions, and it is through user behavior that you can define it. For you to have a full grasp of the permission system on Linux, we may have to discuss more on it.

Permissions
For all the 3 owners discussed above, the 3 permissions below define every directory and file in your Linux system.

- **Execute**: as you can effectively run it, you have an extension ".exe" as an executable program in Windows. However, you won't be able to run an application unless the execute permission is set in Linux. And provided you set permission for write and read, though you can't run it, you might still be able to modify or see the program code.

- **Write**: you will have the influence of editing the contents of a file through the write permission. Also, in the directory, you can rename, remove, and add files as part of the authority you get from the write permission. You can assume where the file is stored, having no permission on the directory, and you have to write permission on file. The file contents can be modified by you. However, removing, moving, or renaming the file from the directory will not be possible for you.

- **Read**: you can read and open a file through the authority given to you by this permission. Also, you can list the content of a directory since you have the read permission.

SSH Command

Mainly, ssh command is included in every Linux system. The SSH client gets started through this command and on a remote machine, enables a secure connection to the SSH server. From a remote machine to logging, the ssh command is used for executing commands on the remote device and transferring files between the two computers.

SSH command in Linux

Over an insecure network and between two hosts, the provision of a secure encrypted connection is made by the ssh command. Also, for tunneling other applications, it can be used for file transfer and terminal access. From a remote location, you can securely run Graphical X11 applications over SSH.

Other SSH commands

With each of them having its page, besides the client ssh, there are other SSH commands.

- sshd – OpenSSH server

- sftp – file transfer with FTP-related command interface

- scp – file transfer with RCP-related command interface

- ssh-add – a tool to add a key to the agent

- ssh –agent – agent to hold private key for single sign-on

- ssh-copy-id – configures a public key as authorized on a server

- ssh-keygen – creates a key pair for public-key authentication

Chapter 9: Linux Terminals, Editors, and Shell

You can find help to get started with the terminal, whether it's been a while you have been using Linux or you are a new user of Linux. Without doubts, a terminal is a powerful tool with lots of values, and it is not something that can scare you. It is not really by reading a single book or article that you will be able to learn everything you need to know about the terminal. Firsthand, to play with the terminal takes experience.

Basic usage of terminal
You will see the bash shell on the application menu of your desktop when you launch a terminal. And by default, bash is what most Linux distributions use even though there are other shells. At the prompt, by typing its name, you can launch a program. Then, it is all a program from command-line utilities to graphical applications such as Firefox concerning everything you launch here. Though those functions are typical of programs, for essential file management, bash has a few built-in commands. And to launch it, you may not need to have the entire path typed to a program, unlike on Windows. For example, you will have to type the whole path to Firefox's .exe file when, on Windows, you attempt to open Firefox. You can type the command below on Linux:

firefox

To run it, after typing a command, go ahead and hit 'enter.' On Linux, programs don't have file extensions, and there's no need to add a .exe or anything else. Also, accepting arguments is part of terminal commands. You can utilize specific types of arguments concerning the program. For example, as arguments, web addresses are accepted by Firefox.

Installing software

Installing software from the terminal is one of the most efficient things to do. The fancy frontend of some terminal commands that they use in the background, such as the Ubuntu Software Center, is the software management applications. Then, you can install them with a terminal background instead of doing it one after the other by selecting and clicking around applications. Also, you can have several apps installed with a distinct command. Since you can see the package management systems by other distributions, you can follow the following command when you intend to install a new software package on Ubuntu:

```
sudo apt-get install packagegename
```

Though it works similar to the Firefox command above, it may appear a bit complicated. With root (administrator) privileges, before launching `apt-get`, `sudo`, you can have the above line launched. Installing a package named `packagegename` is what `packagegename` will install by reading the argument apt-get program. However, it is as arguments that you can also specify multiple packages. For example, you could execute the command below to install Pidgin instant messenger and the Chromium web browser:

```
sudo apt-get install chromium-browser pidgin
```

Also, you could do it with a single command like the above if you want to install all your favorite software after installing Ubuntu. Since you can guess them reasonably quickly, the package names of your preferred programs are all you would need to know. Also, with the help of the tab completion trick, your guesses can be refined.

Text Editors for Linux Desktop

It makes it quite useful for some text editors to also double up as an IDE. Also, they are the default editors. In the Linux environment and for the Linux desktop environment in developing an application, these are quite helpful. The focus

86

will be on a few text editors even though out there, there are a lot of text editors. As such, let's jump right into them:

GNU Emacs

For the Linux environment, one of the oldest text editors is GNU Emacs that has been here for quite some time. GNU's project founder, Richard Stallman, was the one who developed it. All around the world, for thousands of Linux programmers boast of it as their preferred and favorite text editors by using it. With the use of C and LISP, they were able to develop it. To install emacs on Linux Mint or Ubuntu, you can use the commands below:

```
linuxtechi@linuxtechi:~/Downloads$ sudo apt-get update

linuxtechi@linuxtechi:~/Downloads$ sudo apt-get install emacs
```

There are some included unique features of GNU Emacs, which are:

- Extensive support and documentation

- Debugger interface extension

- News and mail options

For Linux Desktop, Atom and *notepadqq* can also be IDE and Text Editors, apart from these text editors.

Nano

In the UNIX operating system, another popular text editor used is Nano. In 2000, it was released, and it is the same as the Pico text editor. Also, to make it as an advanced and powerful text editor, it comes packed with some additional functionality. And it is in the interface only that it can run in a command-line. Here are a few unique features of Nano:

- Autoconf support

- Tab completion

- Auto Indentation

- Case sensitive search

Kwrite

It was in 2000 that Kwrite was first released to the public, and KDE developed this text editor. From KDE, along with the KParts technology, it is entirely based on the text editor for Kate. Making it a more powerful development environment, to a large extent, you can extend the Kwrite's functionality with the help of additional plugin installation. Also, along with encoding your file, it can be used to edit a remote file. On Linux Mint or Ubuntu, to install kwrite, use the command below:

```
linuxtechi@linuxtechi:~/Downloads$ sudo apt-get install
kwrite
```

A few unique features of Kwrite are:

- vi input mode

- Syntax highlighting

- Auto indentation

- Word completion

Eclipse

Eclipse editor can be a suitable option as an advanced and robust editor of code/text for frontend designers and developers. Since it contains several features that support developing and writing Java applications easily, it is entirely in JAVA that it was developed. Also, it is popular among Java developers. For anyone to accomplish extra language support, there may be a requirement for additional plugins if they need it. As the editor can have several advanced functionalities when you insert them with the help of additional plugins, the Eclipse IDE becomes even more powerful. And for the development of programs for COBOL, Ruby on Rails, C++, C, Python, and PHP, you can as well use it. For you to have eclipse installed on Linux Mint or Ubuntu, use the command below:

```
linuxtechi@linuxtechi:~$ sudo apt update

linuxtechi@linuxtechi:~$ sudo apt install eclipse
```

A few of Eclipse's unique features are:

- Plugin support

- For Java developer, tools for Java Development are included

- Open-source and free text editor

Kate
Loaded with the Kubuntu environment, as a default editor, you may have to know about the text editor of Kate if you are familiar with the Kubuntu desktop environment. Given that you can exploit it as a powerful IDE, you also have the opportunity of working with multiple files simultaneously since it is easy to use text editor, it is also a lightweight. Use the command below to install Kate on Linux Mint or Ubuntu:

```
linuxtechi@linuxtechi:~$ sudo apt-get install kate
```

Kate has some exceptional features, and they are:

- Sets indentation for documents automatically

- Auto-detects languages

- Supports several languages

- A powerful IDE

Gedit

Gedit comes loaded by default as a text editor in a GNOME desktop environment. Gedit follows similar objectives as it comes with a simple and clean user interface, and it is lightweight, just as the objective of GNOME to always offer functionalities that are straightforward and clean. With the GNOME desktop environment, getting access to it by the public didn't happen until 2000. It supports entirely for internationalized text as it is completely developed using C language. Gedit possess a few unique features, and they are:

- Supports several programming languages

- Supports internationalized text

- Syntax highlighting

Brackets

For the Linux environment, in 2014, the Brackets was launched by Adobe as a text editor. It has exciting packed features that make working with this editor a lot of fun as an open-sourced text editor. With a clean interface, it is also simple and easy to use. For programmers and web designers to get much-needed help, it is designed as a code editor and also as a text editor. They used JavaScript, CSS, and HTML to develop it completely. With its sophisticated qualities, a few quality text editors may not qualify for all the features it has even as it is on the lightweight side. For the installation on Linux Mint or Ubuntu, you can use the command below:

```
linuxtechi@linuxtechi:~$  sudo add-apt-repository
ppa:webupd8team/brackets

linuxtechi@linuxtechi:~$ sudo apt-get update

linuxtechi@linuxtechi:~$ sudo apt-get install brackets
```

Brackets text editor has a few unique features, which are:

- Focused visual tools Pre-processor support

- Inline editing

- Live preview

Sublime text editor
For the Linux environment, a text editor with so much esteem is a sublime text editor. You can use it as a development environment as well as a text editor; it is packed with several features. Along with various markup languages, it supports a lot of programming. Also, by extending its functionality to a great extent, the many available plugins have made the text editor more sophisticated. You can navigate to any file in your system or easily navigate to the code section through the help of the "Goto Anything" feature, and this is one of the distinctive highlights of this text editor. On Linux Mint or Ubuntu, to install the stable version of the sublime text editor, all you have to do is to refer to some specific commands. A few of the sublime text editor's exclusive elements are:

- Project-specific preferences

- Parallel editing of code

- Python-based plugin API

- Excellent command palette

Geany
For the Linux environment, one relatively recognized text editor that has the integration of the GTK+ toolkit is Geany. For developers and programmers, Geany can also work as an exceptional environment for development. Geany may be a suitable choice for you if you want a development environment and also a text editor. Other packages are not necessary to be installed with it for it to work quite well as it supports nearly all major programming languages and it is lightweight. For the installation of Geany on Linux Mint or Ubuntu, you only need to refer to a particular command. Geany has a few unique features, and they are:

- Interface that is easily pluggable

- Line numbering for easy tracking of code

- Lots of customized options

- Syntax highlighting for easy development

- Clean and easy to use interface

VIM
Vim will be your best choice if you prefer a lot of options and powerful performance to edit your text in an advanced text editor since the default "vi" editor in Linux may appear to bore you. As it is the default Linux text editor's advanced version, the meaning of vim is "vi improved," as suggested by the name. They have the specific need of the developers in mind when they are designing it. Also, for its highly configurable options, it is called a programmer editor. You can use it as a standalone GUI application or as a command-line utility, which is the same as the Vi editor. Here are a few unique features of VIM:

- Automatic commands

- Digraph input

- Split screen

- Session screen

- Tab expansion

- Tag system

- Syntax coloring

Introduction to Linux Shell

You are indirectly interacting with a shell if you are using any major operating system. And every time you use a terminal, you are interacting with a shell if you are running Linux Mint, Ubuntu, or any other Linux distribution. There are a few terminologies that are quite essential before we proceed, and we will discuss them in-depth in the following chapter.

Chapter 10: Basic Linux Shell Commands

On Linux, the command used for analysis is the shell. In a window of terminal emulation, the program users interact with is the shell. On Linux, the workstation's `mate-terminal` GUI is the emulation window. Also, it is an application like `PuTTY` or secure shell client; `SSH` secure on a system with Windows that, around the network, you can register into Linux. In some business or organizational settings, they make use of the Bourne Again Shell, `bash`. If you prefer, you can choose from some of the available shells like the TC-Shell, C-Shell, as well as the Bourne Shell. As specific features are appropriate to each of them, they all boast of the same characteristics. The features below belong to bash:

- As it remembers the last few commands, the history mechanism of the shell is indeed functional. In addition to a reference number, to list the previous few commands, you can make use of the `history` command.

For you to rerun a command, you can cut and paste from the history in a terminal emulation window of a workstation. Also, to rerun any command from history, the symbol `i` can be used.

- There is also "job control" for the shell, and in the background, you can run any programs that don't require any terminal interaction.

Available straightaway for other commands is the shell and the program `sort` in the background. In this case, the job control number "1" is printed by the shell as well as "3470," which is the process identity number. As it is running in the foreground, you can also use the special character Ctrl + z to suspend a program. You can then use `fg` to continue it in the foreground and even the `bg` command to put the program in the background. You can refer to them by their job number if there is more than one running program in the background or suspended. As such, use the `jobs` command to list the status of all stopped or background jobs to see your jobs and their job numbers.

- You can write the scripts of shell commands, and similar to the compiled programs, you can invoke them as such by merely naming them. For example, we can first create a file in ~/bin containing the specific command to create a script that counts the number of C program files in this recent directory.

Before running it like normal, we can use the `chmod` command to make the file executable.

- With *if-then-else* statements, *for* loops, and *while* loops, bash is an interpretive programming language. When you type the command below, you will get more details about the Linux on-line documentation:

- The shell possesses numeric and string-valued variables.

The directory for home is `$HOME` as pre-set for some variables, and to see a list of assigned variables, type the `set` command.

- You can find it cumbersome to enter, or for the frequent execution of specific commands or groups of commands; you may want to assign *aliases*. For example, in a recent directory, to have the number of files of C program counted, we can assign an alias "countc" for the number counting of lines output using *wc* and have the files listed using *ls*.

- To *pipe* one program's output to another program's input, the shell boasts of such a facility. "| " is the symbol of the pipe. For example, in the `wc` program, we may have the output piped after we might have `cat` the file for us to count the number of words in file A.

- The *standard output* and *standard input* are the concept that most Linux programs and commands observe. An onslaught of output written by the program is the average output, and a flood of data read by the programs is the standard input. Most times, accompanying the terminal is most of these so that your screen can get this output while it is from your keyboard that you get the input. You can have the standard *redirected* to output and input through the shell.

- In your recent directory, to match filenames, the shell will expand the wildcards. For example, you can use a specific command to give a directory listing of the file with names "`anything.c`"

- Filenames are represented by the *argument* strings that the commands have. For example, in your home directory, the command can change the current directory to "`bin,`" and the meaning of *tilde* is that the shell is your home directory.

- For it to identify it, the process entails verifying to discover the built-in element is connected to the command and may then explore for a collection of directories by typing in a command name. The *search path* is what this means and included in the current directory is the search path, its subdirectory "bin," and your home directory. And through typing their names, you may invoke them after you must have written your programs. No matter what your current directory is, if in the directory, you deposit such a program, it will be found and then run.

- By naming them, you can invoke commands. Most Linux commands are just programs that the shell executes. For example, the command ls can list the names of its files and read the recent directory as you get a specific result when you run it.

- There is an associated current directory that, similar to other programs, the shell has. When locating files, as the starting point, programs running on Linux use the current directory. In the filesystem of Linux, getting a different location by changing the recent directory is possible by using the cd command of the shell.

- The user can configure this command prompt. A dollar symbol preceded by "bash," as well as the version number of the bash program, is the default prompt.

With the use of the up-arrow keyboard, you can use previous commands of edit and recall with the help of an additional mechanism of bash. On top of the terminal, the final command will re-appear once you push the up-arrow, and to get the earlier commands, press the up-arrow once more. Hit on "RETURN" to have the command replayed. You can insert characters within the command or to delete by repositioning the cursor with the use of the key for back-arrow or from the end, remove characters by using the delete key to amend the command before rerunning it.

Shell Commands

Below, you will find a summary of the commands available. For each command, the reference on the manual page can give you more details. The command `man` can be used after your preferred name to see these online.

Database management
Available are Oracle and MySQL

Command	Description
MySQL-workbench	GUI interface for MySQL
Sqldeveloper	Oracle SQL Developer GUI interface
Mysql	Run the MySQL SQL interface
Sqlplus	Run the Oracle SQL interpreter

Word processing
LibreOffice is available and compatible with Microsoft Office.

Command	Description
LibreOffice	start applications for LibreOffice

Load at Antichi Colli EURU1269036 For developing high-quality printed documents using Linux or other operating systems, an extensively used language of typesetting is `TeX`. When you intend to format manual pages, the standard typical Linux

text formatting people generally use is another program
collection built on `Troff`.

TeX

Command	Description
Dvips	Convert a DVI file to POST SCRIPT
Xdvi	DVI previewer
Pdflatex	latex formatter with PDF output
latex	latex formatter
tex	text formatting and typesetting

Troff

Command	Description
Pic	troff preprocessor for drawing pictures
groff	GNU troff interface for laserprinting
nroff	text formatting language
troff	text formatting and typesetting language
Grap	pic preprocessor for drawing graphs
tbl	prepare tables for nroff or troff
eqn	mathematical preprocessor for troff

General commands

Command	Description
aspell	interactive spelling checker
spell	check text for spelling error
acroread	PDF viewer
evince	GNOME PostScript previewer
fmt	simple text formatter

Programming

Available are these languages and programming tools.

FORTRAN

Command	Description
f95	GNU Fortran 95 compiler

JAVA

Command	Description
eclipse	Java integrated development environment on Linux
javac	JAVA compiler
appletviewer	JAVA applet viewer

C++

Command	Description
g++	GNU C++ Compiler

C

Command	Description
cxref	generate C program cross reference
indent	indent and format C program source
ctrace	C program debugger
gcc	GNU ANSI C Compiler
cb	C program beautifier

General

Command	Description
strip	remove symbol table and relocate bits
nm	print program's name list
Size	print program's size
make	maintain groups of programs

Other languages (not on all systems are these available)

Command	Description
asp	web page embedded language
mathematica	symbolic maths package
php	web page embedded language
squeak	Smalltalk

python	object-oriented programming language
perl	general purpose language
gcl	GNU Common Lisp
mattab	maths package
bc	interactive arithmetic language processor

Networking

Command	Description
google-chrome	web browser
firefox	web browser
curl	transfer data from a url
rsh	remote shell
rlogin	gaining access remotely to a Linux host
ssh	secure shell terminal or command connection
telnet	getting to another host by connecting through the terminal
wget	non-interactive network downloader
scp	copy of remote file for secure shell
rcp	remote file copy
sftp	program for transferring file in secure shell

tftp	trivial file transfer program
ftp	file transfer program

Messages between users

There is support for on-screen messages to other users and world-wide electronic mail in the Linux systems.

Command	Description
thunderbird	GUI mail handling tool on Linux
Mail	mail program for easy read or send
pine	vdu-based mail utility
wall	send a message to all local users

Printing

Expect the printer name to be given following a $-p$ argument as most commands which can be used to print files. And as simple text files, files may be sent to the printers or for the laser printers; they may be processed in various ways.

Command	Description
a2ps-P*printer*	format text file in PostScript and print on laser printer
dvips-P*printer*	postprocess TeX file into PostScript and print on a laser printer
LPR-P*printer*	send a file to a printer

Direct from some applications or with the use of the GUI print manager; you can use the shell to print files. It is by name that you need to specify a printer, and some of them are:

Printer Name	Location
tl4_lw	Teaching Lab 4 (C/2.10) laser printer
tl2_lw	Teaching Lab 2 (C/2.05) laser printer
tl3_lw	Teaching Lab 3 (C/2.08) laser print
tl1_lw	Teaching Lab 1 (C/2.04) laser printer

Status

These commands alter or list information about the system.

Command	Description
printenv	display value of a shell variable
who	list logged in users
w	show what logged in users are doing
netstat	show network status
vmstat	report virtual memory statistics
lun	list user names or login ID
users	print names of logged-in users
last	show last logins of users

uptime	display system status
kill	send a signal to a process
Tty	print current terminal name
iostat	report I/O statistics
homequota	show quota and file usage
time	time a command
groups	show group memberships
stty	Set terminal options
script	keep script of terminal session
du	print amount of disk usage
reset	reset terminal mode
quota −v	display disk usage and limits
date	print the date
ps	print process status statistic

Information
Here are some shell commands that give information.

Command	Description
yelp	GNOME help viewer
info	displays command information pages online
man	displays manual pages online

apropos	locate commands by keyword lookup

Compressed files

To save space, you may need to compress files. You can use the following to examine and create compressed files.

Command	Description
zcmp, zdiff	compare compressed files
gunzip	uncompress gzipped files
zcat	cat a compressed file
uncompress	uncompress files
zmore	file perusal filter for crt viewing of compressed text
gzip	compress files

Manipulating data

You can use the command below to alter or compare the contents of files.

Command	Description
wc	count characters, lines, and words
look	find lines in sorted data
join	join files on some common field
uniq	report repeated lines in a file
gawk	pattern processing and scanning language

tr	translate characters
expand, unexpand	expand tabs to spaces and vice versa
split	split file into smaller files
diff	differential file comparator
sort	sort file data
cut	cut out selected fields of each line of a file
sed	stream text editor
comm	compare sorted data
paste	merge file data
cmp	compare the contents of two files
perl	data manipulation language
awk	Pattern processing and scanning language

File editors
You can amend and create files by using editors.

Command	Description
vi, vim	standard text editor
gedit	GNOME text editor
pluma	Mate GUI text editor
pico	easy text editor for vdus
ex, edit	line editor

| xemacs | emacs with mouse action |
| emacs | GNU project Emacs |

Files directory

You can handle files and create file directory through these commands.

Command	Description
lpq	spool queue examination program
touch	update modification and access times of a file
just	text justification program
tail	print last lines from file
head	give first few lines
rm, rmdir	remove (unlink) directories or files
grep	search file for regular expression
pwd	print working directory
find	Find files
mv	rename or move file type
file	determine file type
more, page	display file data at your terminal
cp	copy file data
mkdir	make a new directory

chmod	change file mode
ls	list and generate statistics for files
chgrp	change file group
lprm, cancel	Remove jobs from line printer queue
cd	change current directory
lpr	spool file for line printing

Logging out

Command	Description
logout	log out of a Linux terminal

You must take note that you must exit the Desktop Environment instead of a Linux workstation.

Chapter 11: Shell Scripting

For a Linux-based OS, a text file that has commands sequence is a shell script. The commands sequence of the shell script would have to be typed into a single script at a time into the keyboard. As an interpreter for commands set that you use to communicate with the system, the shell is the CLI, command-line interface's operating system. For them to save time, a user must repeatedly use the command sequence of a shell script. There are subcommands, comments, and parameters that the shell needs to follow, just like other programs. And it is by entering the file name on a command-line in the shell that users can initiate the sequence of commands. A shell script is known as a batch file in the DOS operating system as it also referred to as an EXEC in the mainframe VM operating system of IBM.

You can enter the command for the system execution since it is within the operating system of Linux that you will find the shell program. On a Linux computer, the shell program will start, providing the chance to have your commands entered through an interface when a terminal window is opened. The command-line interface is what this interface is referred to by people. On the screen, you can see the display of the output, and the shell executes it when a command is entered. Also, stored in a file, some commands can also be executed by the shell in addition to being able to execute and accept commands interactively. Shell scripting is recognized as the mode of this execution.

How shell script works
Giving the shell executive permission, making the script accessible to the shell, and writing the script are some of the fundamental steps involved with shell scripting. You can use a graphical user interface, GUI, word processor, or text editor to write shell script since it contains ASCII. The shell can interpret the language of a series of commands in the content of the script. Shortcuts, arrays, *if/then/else* statements, variables, and loops are some of the functions

that shell scripts support. In a location that the shell can access, you can use the .sh or .txt extension to save the file once complete.

Background to the shell

In the 1970s, Ken Thomson developed V6 Shell, a shell program to start with Unix. Its scripting proficiency was quite lacking even as it was a shell with interactive features. In 1977, Bourne Shell came on board and for the root account; as the default shell, it remains in use today. And through the years, it has been quite useful through the scripting abilities. By the 80s, Korn Shell and C-Shell gave the public something to talk about as the highly popular shell variants. There was a drastic difference from the original shell as specific syntax has been brought by every one of these shells. As such, Bash is an extremely prominent shell today. As the unique Bourne Shell's massively enhanced variant, it stands for Bourne-Again- Shell.

Shell script applications examples

By typing one line at a time, you can save quite a lot of time from doing some repetitive task when you use a shell script. Below are some of the examples of applications that you can use a shell script for:

- Monitoring a system

- Executing routine backups

- Linking existing programs together

- Manipulating files

- Completing batch

- Creating a program or running a programming environment

- Automating the code compiling process

Shell script execution

As the shell's argument, all you have to do is to pass the script path if you want to execute a shell script. You need to pay attention to the fact that LF characters, Line-Feed, are required for terminating the lines by the shell. It is easy to run into errors if, on a Linux system, you attempt to execute shell script promptly or write it on Windows. For line termination, Carriage-return-Line-Feed, the combination of CR-LF is what Windows uses, and you will need to have it in LF-only conversion. For means to go about achieving this, you can check your Windows editor.

As a command, the shell script can be executed directly using another way. As your shell script's first line, you can insert the *hashbang* declaration below:

```
#!/bin/bash
```

Then, you can do some command to make your script file executable. Right now, without having to reference the shell explicitly, you can have the script file executed directly.

Benefits of shell scripts

Things are meant to be efficient and simple when you use shell script. It removes any interpretation issues since it is a similar syntax that it uses on the shell command-line that it uses in the script. Also, more than other programming languages, it requires less of learning curves and also faster when it comes to writing code for a shell script. However, if left unnoticed, this tends to prove extremely costly if there is an error in a shell script. Also, there may not be compatibility with different platforms connected with shell scripting, and more than individual commands; shell scripts can also be slower to execute. All the same, here are more advantages of shell scripts.

Portable:

When the shell itself is present, you can transfer a shell script to another Unix and Unix-related OS. Also, shell scripts are much more portable than C/C++ programs when you are in the process of transferring a shell script from different architectures like Sparc, MIPS, x86, and so on. You will have to attempt to run a C/C++, build the program, and copy the source code for you to transfer and use a C/C++ program. Then, if it uses the architecture-specific code, it may not work as expected.

Transparency:

Since it is a text file, you can check out the kind of actions the shell script is performing by viewing it quite easily. By contrast, it is if you have access to the source code or the source code wants to inform you that you can know the type of program in a language like C/C++. For example, it is possible to find out if any files are getting deleted by a shell script and then have those files copied to another place if you need those files. Also, because you may gain access to view the source code, shell scripts can be quite simple to diagnose than the regular programs. Though to avoid such errors, creating and checking programs are some of the responsibilities of a compliant shell script. You can as well create the directory as you look in the script code.

Easier to develop:

Inside a regular program written in C/C++, you can efficiently perform similar actions as the shell script. However, the shell script can be debugged and written far easier than a program like C/C++. By redirecting output, removing directories and files, and also execution of external commands, the shell is great for all these specific system administration tasks and more. For a much lower level operation, including manipulating data structures, invoking system calls, and so on, C/C++ programs tend to be much suitable for them.

Multiple commands combination:

One of the benefits of shell scripting is you can have multiple distinct sequences of commands as well as automating frequent tasks. For you to remember the direction in which you can execute multiple commands can be quite challenging than a single command. The Linux OS system sequence of boot-up is a perfect example here. For it to get the system into a proper state, the operating system executes a series of commands as one aspect of the boot-up process. The shell scripts that exist in the directory /etc are these commands. You may end up performing the process by hand in the absence of shell scripts, and a system booting process complexity will come to your realization if you take a look at these shell scripts types. The /etc/profile is an example of a shell script, and with the access of a user into the system, it can thus be executed.

Task automation:

Your executed tasks can be frequently automated when you use shell scripts, and this is the first benefit of it. Let's assume that daily, you need to perform a set of tasks. You can run these commands on the script after storing them in a file when you have to execute multiple commands on your Linux daily. For example:

- For too low or too high prices, when specific conditions are met, trigger an SMS or email as you parse the fetched data or fetch stock prices.

- As some log files appear to be growing every day, you can compress them.

- You can upload and archive a folder or file to a cloud storage facility every day like S3.

Features of Shell Scripting

Shell scripting is powerful

For every Linux-based operating system, you can get help almost for every one of them without any complaint, and it is convenient. You will have an excellent basis when you marge it with the standard accessible tool such as `sed`, `grep`, and `awk`.

Readability

It is much lower to develop anything that is unreadable with a shell script. You can certainly make use of some unique features of the shell that others do not know of them.

Regularly accessible

On all the programs you come across, you can always use shell scripting. By automating repetitive steps, it makes your life quite easier. All you need do is to insert your preferred commands in a file and run it happily after making it executable. As it is quick to master, so it is quite simple to learn.

Repeating

In your shell script, you don't need recurring similar statements every day. Create a compelling set of functions and consist of that in your existing and new shell scripts. While you can call your function "Display," resist it when you are about to use "echo."

Conclusion

To write workflow for epsilon, ETL, and several other tools to save time, quite useful for many organizations, is the scope of the shell scripts. And with the use of any of the shell scripts, professionals and users of Linux who want to automate tasks on Linux are the target audience of learning shell scripting technologies. For conditional programs that contain limited functions, loops, and statements, shell scripts can help to create these complex programs. Also, you can store data with shell scripts.

Chapter 12: Building Script

Using the language of programming for the shell are short programs, while the interpretation can be achieved through the shell scripts and a process of the shell. On Linux and other operating systems, they are quite ideal for task automation. For Unix-related OS, a program that provides the text-only, traditional interface is a shell program. You can read commands that you type into a terminal window as an all-text mode window, as well as console, which is an all-text display mode, and then run its primary function. The very common versatile and highly used *bash* is the default shell on Linux as groups of commands that you can translate, which is compiled or interpreted into a machine language form, and that can be wholly understood by the system's CPU, the central processing unit. You write computer programs with artificial, precise language, which is a programming language.

To create shell scripts, shell scripting language or shell programming language are the bash feature, and other Unix-related OS use shells with each of them containing the programming language with built-in features. You can easily have shell scripts created, and when you go online and in several books are available for a comprehensive selection of undertakings with or without notification. These factors are some of the advantages of using shell scripts. Also, in the Unix-related OS default installation, shell scripts are used extensively.

The first script
Here, you will see a useful introduction to shell scripts handling and creation with the following example. All previous lines of the screen of your monitor are cleared by the script, and on it, the text, *Good morning, world,* is written by it. You may not need a word processor but only need to have a text editor like *vi* or *gedit* opened when you want to create this script.

Also, with the functions of copy and paste used in the standard keyboard, you can copy the above code, open the text editor, and paste it into it. Then, the script is complete and quite close to running it after you have given a name to the file and have this plain text saved. By having the file name after a forward slash and a dot typed without any spaces between them and then hit on the 'enter' button, you will be ready to run scripts. For example, you can use the command below in the attempt to run it if you have the above script saved as *morning*:

```
./morning
```

Nevertheless, since you must first set the file to be *executable*, on the screen, you can see the message of error. In that situation, the script will not run. For the new files, *write* and *read* are the only permissions they have by default. With its option of *755*, you can make use of the chmod command to easily solve the problem. Using this, however in the same directory as the one below, you will have the ability not only to write and read the file, but you can also execute it:

```
chmod 755 morning
```

Then, while in the same directory and by typing the command below, you can prepare to run the script. To continue, hit the 'enter' button:

```
./morning
```

The operation process
The type of shell to use for the interpretation of the script and for locating the shell is the first three lines will tell the operating systems. As the directory */bin* is its location, the shell is bash, and as such, the */bin/bash* is what the line contains. For the operating system to receive its signal that it is offering the shell's location and name and other scripting languages, an exclamation mark, and a pound sign always precedes this instruction.

For you to dispense the command `clear`, it is the second line that the shell informs. With this easy command, you can remove all previous output and commands from the terminal or console window that there is a release of the command. On the screen, the *Good morning, world* phrase is what the shell gets from the third line. For whatever follows it to be repeated from the shell instruction, it uses the *echo* command. In a more advanced script, the quotation marks can make a big difference to use them as a useful programming drill even though they may not be necessary. An input data, an *argument* that the command `echo` receives is the *Good morning, world*, which is in slightly more technical terms. Also, scripts that people use freely are `echo` and `clear`, as is the case with other commands. For example, you will get the prompt to enter the next command, and you will have the entire previous output and commands removed when you type *clear* on the screen and hit the 'enter' button.

It isn't working!
There can be some reasons for the phrase *Good morning, world* not to appear at the top of the screen and some of them are:

1. For the *owner* of the file, they forget to change the permissions to *execute*.

2. In the same directory, the command was not issued where the file is located.

3. Instead of a text editor, a word processor was used to create it, and as such, the file is not a plain text file.

4. After the slash or period, space was inserted.

5. In the command, you omit or reverse the forward-slash or the period.

6. There is a difference in the name of the file and the one used in the command. For example, there can be

a difference between capitalization, spelling, or even an extra or minor space.

7. You omit the word `echo`, and as a result, you made an error as you attempt to copy the code.

As the administrative user or the root, it is vital not to practice executing and writing scripts. You can damage the operating system with an improperly written script. Also, it could lead to necessarily reinstalling the operating system as a whole and result in the loss of valuable data in the worst-case scenario. You can easily use a command like `adduser` to quickly create one if an ordinary user account does not yet exist on the computer because of this reason.

Experiments
Before you make a move to more complicated examples, if you are a curious user, you can do a variety of instructive, simple experiments. With the suggestions below, they make up of code revision, using a different file name or a similar name of a file to save the changes, and then with the above explanation, executing them.

1. Attempt to have a few of the wording altered. For instance, have the line changed to *"Good morning, people!"* `echo`.

2. For the line that you will write on the screen, you can have a line, or more additional lines added as one horizontal space follow them at in any case, with each beginning having the word `echo`.

3. Concerning both lines of `echo`, you can also leave an empty line. Though by having `echo` typed on it, you can create a blank line, and that is all. It will be seen that this will not affect the result.

4. Then, have blank horizontal spaces inserted. Based on if you enter the primary reference marks before or after, there will be a different result.

5. To have a different location directory for the execution of the file. As such, when it is issued, you will have to add to the command name beginning, the executable script path. For example, if you have moved the file to `test`, a term of a subdirectory, you will have `./test/morning`.

6. You will want to add to the script file, some other command as another experiment like `df` that reveals the disk space usage, `uname`, which gives information about the hardware and software of a system, `pwd` that informs the present directory, and `ps` that explains the processes currently on the system. It is vital to understand that with any appropriate arguments or options, you can use these as well as other commands within the script.

Hello, World!
For you to have the shell script created:

1. *vi* is the text editor suitable for you to use for this, and within the file, have in its logic and commands of Linux that you required.

2. You will need to escape from vi, and before doing so, close after saving the file.

3. The executable form of the script is quite essential

4. Then, you can move on to the environment of production once the output satisfies you after testing the script.

5. A line in Bash, which is a straightforward program, informs a command of the computer. So, use your preferred text editor like vi to start it.

Necessary Commands of vi:

- To vacate vi:

```
Type :q after pressing ESC
```

- To search for a string:

```
type /wordToSearch after pressing ESC
```

- To jump to a line:

```
type :the line number after pressing ESC
```

- To quit after saving a file:

```
type :x after pressing ESC
```

OR

```
type :wq after pressing ESC
```

- To store a file:

```
type :w filename after pressing ESC
```

- To go into command mode:

```
press ESC
```

- To go into edit mode:

```
type I after pressing ESC
```

- To open a file:

```
vi filename
```

The script running after saving it
On the screen, a message of error is what the `./hello.sh`
command displayed. Since for the `hello.sh` script, you
have not set executed permission, it may end up not running
the script.

Chmod command
To change the access permission of a file, you can make use
of the chmod command. As follows, below is the syntax:

```
chmod ugo+rwx filename
```

Where:

- x: execute permission

- w: write permission

- r: read permission

- =: overwrite current permissions

- -: removes the permission

- +: adds the permission

- o: others

- g: groups

- u: users

Below is how you can express permission through a numerical way:

- 0: no permissions at all

- 7: read, write, and execute permissions

- 1: execute permission

- 2: write permission

- 4: read permission

Errors

The *robustness* of the program is often the measure used to differentiate a good and inadequate program. As such, when things go wrong, this is the ability of the program to handle these circumstances.

Exit status

When it finishes, returning to the exit condition is what every program that is well-written does. Zero will be the exit status when a program completes quite successfully. Then, in some way, the program failed if there is nothing more than zero for the exit status. For the program exit status in the scripts that you call, it is entirely vital to check them. Also, when they finish, there must be a meaningful return on the exit status of your scripts. Specific lines of code like $some_directory can be written for the creation system by the system administrator of a Unix.

If everything goes quite well enough, this way might not have been the wrong way of going about doing this. To the name that the $some_directory contained, the working directory was changed by the two lines and also in such a directory, delete the file. That is quite the projected action. And if the named directory in that $some_directory doesn't exist, what will then happen? Then, on the directory that is currently operational, the script will have the command rm executed and the command cd will fail. Indeed, not the planned action!

The exit category check

For you to respond and get the program's exit status, you can use several ways. First, the environment alternative of the $? and its contents require adequate observation and for the execution of the last command is an exit status that the $? will contain.

Except to revert zero's exit status and also one respectively, the false and true commands are programs that remain dormant. And for the previous program, the exit position is what is contained in the $? environment option. Hence, it is quite essential to have the exit category checked.

The cd command's exit level is examined in this variety, and on standard error, we can have the error message printed if it's not zero and with 1 as the exit status, have the script terminated. However, we can save ourselves a few typing efforts by using some smarter techniques even when this happens to be an effective way-out to the crisis. Since it is the given commands of the exit status that it evaluates, we can make use of the statement `if` precisely as the next approach to attempt.

If there's a success with the command `cd`, we can check it here. And for the indication that an error has happened, a code of 1 is the program exit. As for the output is the error message, you can then execute `rm`.

Chapter 13: Basic Bash Shell Commands

In a circumstance that a directory tends to be a *root directory* by possessing no parent directory or within a single other directories, it is a *subdirectory* that is known as "parent." Thus, modern filesystems have folder or directory trees. And you can always get to the root directory by going from child directory to parent directory, which is typical of traversing backward through the file tree. Though Unix and Unix-like system only have \., a single root directory, such as Windows' drives: *A:* \, *C:* \, etc., some filesystems have multiple root directories.

```
pwd / ls / cd
```

As we refer to the *working directory* or the current directory, it is always within some directories that the user is always using when working within a filesystem. With `pwd`, print the working directory of the user. Using `ls`, make a list of files and child directories, etc., that is, the content of this directory. Here, you need to pay attention to some of these points:

- Instead of `ls -l -a`, you can sometimes chain flag like `ls -la`
- Have a combination of several flags such as `ls -l -a`
- Reveal file details with `ls -l`
- Using `ls -a` to reveal hidden ("dot") files

Using cd (change directory) to change to a different directory and the parent directory, the shorthand for `cd` is `cd`. To home directory normally /home/username or similar directory, the shorthand for `cd ~` or simply cd is `cd`. For this directory, `cd.` may not make any much impact since `.` is shorthand. Use `cd` `-` to go back to the most recent directory. And by using `cd` `../,,,etc.`, you can jump multiple directories levels. To home directory user, `cd` `~user` means `cd`.

; / && / &

Commands are the things that you type into the command-line and stored somewhere on your computer; they always execute some machine code. Sometimes, a built-in Linux command is this machine code, and sometimes also, it is some code that you wrote yourself and perhaps an app. Occasionally, right after another, we will want to run one command, and we can as well use the ";" (semicolon) to do that:

The meaning of the semicolon is `l` first `(ls)` lists the contents of the working directory, and then `l` `(pwd)` prints its location. Then, `&&` can be used to chain commands, which is another useful tool. If the command to the left fails, the command to the right will not run. On the same line, you can use both `&&` and `;` multiple times.

Even if the first one fails, the second will run with `;`. There is a completely different function fulfilled by & even when it looks similar to &&. Usually, before it gives you access to enter another one, the command-line will wait for that command to finish when you execute a long-running command. You will be able to perform a new command while an older one is still going and also prevents this from happening when you put & after a command.

It is essential to know that we assume that the process or job is "*backgrounded*" when, to hide it, we make use of `&` after a command. Then, use the `job` command to see what background jobs are currently running.

Getting Help

man

For you to bring manual for that command (with *q*, quit *man*), type man before nearly any command.

-h

And for you to bring up a help menu for that command, type *--help* or *-h*.

Viewing and editing files

nano / nedit

For people or beginners that want to learn a million shortcuts, as a command-line text editor with minimalistic characteristics, nano is a great editor. For the first few years of coding career, it will be sufficient for any developer or programmer. As it allows for syntax highlighting, drag-and-drop, point-and-click editing, nedit opens up an X Window as a small graphical editor. When you plan to make some changes to a script and then rerun it over, you may want to use nedit for that. Atom, Notepad++, gedit, vim, vi, emacs, and some others are other common editors like graphical user interface, GUI or command-line interface, CLI. Others are VS Code, Light Table, and Micro. The syntax highlighting, search and replace, and some other things are the basic convenience that all modern editors provide. Though nano and nedit don't have as many more features as emacs and vi(m), their learning curves tend to be much steeper. You will discover the one that works for you after trying out a few different editors.

head / tail / cat / less

File's few first lines are the `head` outputs. Though the default is 10, the number of lines to show is specified by the -n flag. File's last few lines are the `tail` outputs. Beginning from the N -th line with *tail -n +N*, you can get the end of the file or, like above, you can get the last n lines. Usually, the terminal, but what sends files to the standard output stream and concatenates a list of files is `cat`. You can use it to view files quickly, and with multiple files or just a single file, you can make use of the `cat`. But, here, pay close attention; you may be accused of a UUOC, Useless Use of Cat if you use `cat` in this way. You may not worry yourself too much about that because it's not a big deal.

For you to quickly view a file, another tool is `less` as it opens vim —like, read-only window. `more` is another command. However, `less` has a higher recommendation than `more` since it provides a superset of the functionality of `more`. At their `man` pages, you can learn about `more` and `less`.

Creating and deleting directories and files

mkdir / rm / rmdir

For you to create new, empty directories, you can use *mkdir*. As this is non-recoverable, you need to be cautious as using `rm` can remove any file. Then, with the *-i* flag, an *"are you sure?"* prompt can be removed. With the use of `rmdir`, you can remove an empty directory. Then, you could see a reference to its parent directory (..) as well as a reference to the directory itself (.) when you *ls -a* in an empty directory. It is only empty directories that `rmdir` removes.

However, using *rm -rf* (*-r* = recursive, *-f* =force) cannot remove a directory and all of its content.

touch

It is to modify file timestamps that `touch` was created. However, you can also create an empty file using it and such as `nano`, by opening it with a text editor, you can create a new file. You can also edit the file. Also, `touch` can be used as well. Note: ^z (Ctrl+z) is the background a process. Then, hit ^z with editing file. Shown by the jobs command where *N* is the job index, use `kill %N` to kill a background process. While it is running, press ^c (Ctrl+c) to kill the current (foreground) from processing.

History of command, links making, and copying and making files

mv / cp / ln

To rename or move a file, use `mv`. You can `mv` a file to a new file, to rename it, or keep the same file or `mv` a file to a new directory. Then, copy a file using *cp*. And for you to create a hard link to a file, use *ln*. Also, you can get a soft link created to a file with *ln -s*. In memory that contains a file, the same actual bytes are referenced in hard links, and while it points to those bytes, the soft links refer to the original fine name.

Command history

For you to be able to rerun and complete commands, there are two main features that you can get from `bash`. *Tab completion* is the first feature. For guessing the precise action you are attempting to take, you only need to press the key <tab> after you have the first section of the command typed. Then, you will complete the command after you must have typed *ls t* and press the TAB key. Note that if an ambiguity case arises, it may be required of you to press the <tab> several times. And as for your previously typed commands, you can get the short history of them since bash keeps them, and by typing ^r(Ctrl+r), you will have the chance to have a search through for those commands. If you want to see the command history search, hit ^r(Ctrl+r).

Processes, disk usage, and directory trees
ps / du / df

For the hard drives of your system or the disks, if you want to know the amount of space your files have taken up, df will be there to show you. If you go through this command, you will notice that the meaning of −h is "human-readable" and not "help." And rather than writing out integer, huge bytes number, to display disk or file sizes, it is G for gigabytes and K for kilobytes that some commands use. For the subdirectories of a specific directory, the file space usage is what the du shows. You may use df for you to discover the free space of a particular hard drive. Also, using du will allow you to know the quantity of a directory's space. From the specified directory, the flag --max-depth=N are directories N levels fewer or down, which du takes. For current processes running by the users, it is shown by the ps.

tree/ mkdir -p

It is only a single directory, by default, that mkdir makes. As such, using mkdir only, it may be hard for you to make *d/e/f* since *d/e* directory has no existence. And also, if there is no such existence for them, all directories in the path can be made when we pass to mkdir from the -p. Also, when we have a nicely-formatted directory printed, we can visualize the structure of a directory better through the help of the tree. With a specified directory, in the beginning, the whole structure of the tree is printed by it. However, using the flag -L, you will have the power of restricting it to a particular number of levels. Then, using -prune, in the output of the tree, the empty directory can be hidden. You must know that the directory that is not that empty or the "recursive empty" will also be removed by this command, but which has in them other recursively empty directories or other empty directories.

Miscellaneous
exit / logout / passwd

You can use `passwd` to have the password of your account changed. To verify it, you may have to provide the current password you are using. Then, to forestall any typo situation, it will want you to enter your new password two times. In a situation where it is only a user account that you have, the shell you have logged in will exit with the use of `logout`. And to have any shell exited, then use the `exit`.

*clear / ***

For you to have your new terminal line moved on to the screen top, then run `clear`. Below the line of your current prompt, you will have blank lines added to them by this command. Thus, you can clear your workspace with this. And in the situation of looking for specific files, wildcard, also known as Kleene Star, *, is perfect for it. And since it is equivalent to more characters or zero, in a command, you can make use of the glob several times.

Processor usage, memory, and disk
htop / top

The processes that are running recently as well as their memory usage, owners, and many can be displayed through the `top`. The variant of the `top`, which is interactive and enhanced, is an `htop`. You need to know that the display processes can be restricted by using a `username` only to those owners while passing the flag `-u username`.

ncdu

Typical of an enhanced `du`, it is the file space usage overview, which is navigable that the `ncdu` offers. Also, it is a `vim`-related window with a read-only feature that it can open. When you want to quite, press `q`.

REPLs
Though they utilize it for specific programming languages, typical of the command-line is Real-Evaluate-Print Loop, which is REPL. While you can use the function `quit()` for

you to quit, the command `python` is what you can use to open the Python REPL. Also, using the command `R`, you can have the R REPL opened as well as using the function `q()` for you to quit. With the command `scala`, you can also have the Scala REPL opened and the command `:quit` when you want to quit. With Java REPL, you can use command `jshell` to have it opened and `/exit` command for you to quit. Optionally, with the use of `^d(Ctrl+d)`, you can exit any of the REPLs. As `^d` signifies the input's end on Unix, it is also the marker for the end of the file, EOF.

-v / --version / -version

For most programs and commands to have the software version, they possess the flag `--version` or `-version`. This information tends to be available easily for most applications, even though there is a less intuitive factor for most. You need to take notice of the use of `-v` by some programs for the version flag, and this means 'verbose' for using `-v` by others, which, while debugging information or printing several diagnostics, can run the application.

Environment variables

Within your `bash` shell, the tenacious variables that you can use and create are the environment variable, and "env vars" is their short-term. You can use it with the sign of a dollar (`$`), and for their definition, they make use of the equal sign (`=`). When you use `printenv`, the entire recently-defined env vars can be seen. Using the sign =, you can have a new environment variable set. You must be careful to note that your = has no space after or before. Using `echo` with a preceding sign of `$`, you can have a particular env var printed to the terminal. Attempt to surround other whitespace or all spaces around the environment variables with the quotes ("..."). Also, be cautious because you won't get any warning and will probably overwrite an env var by having a value reassigned to it. Apart from those above, you can also use the command `export` to define the env vars. Also, they can be available to sub-processes, which are commands you called from this shell when you provide the meaning this way. When you use the command `unset` or leave the right-hand side of the = blank, you can have the environment variables unset.

Chapter 14: Advanced Bash Shell Commands

As a fairly powerful programming language and not only appropriating seam connecting the user and the kernel of the operating system, the shell is a command interpreter. And by *gluing* together compiled binaries, utilities, tools, and system calls, you can build applications through a straightforward device called a script inside a shell program. By a shell script, available for invocation are indeed the whole catalog of Unix tools, utilities, and commands. Also, there can be additional flexibility and power to scripts through external shell commands like loop and testing constructs, if that were not enough. Without requiring a complete compactly designed programming language with plenty of the bells and whistles, it is to administrative systems tasks as well as other routines, repetitive jobs that shell scripts exceptionally lend themselves.

Introduction to Regular Expression

A sequence of characters is an expression. Metacharacters are those characters that have an interpretation beyond and above the factual connotation that they have. For example, a speech by someone may be denoted by a quote symbol and ditto the subsequent symbols for a meta-meaning. Metacharacters or characters that specify or match patterns are regular expressions. Here are some of the components that a regular expression contains:

- **Modifiers**. By modifying, for the range of text that the regular expression is to match, these narrow or expand it. The backlash, brackets, and asterisk are some of the modifiers.

- **An anchor**. For the match between the text line and the regular expression, it is the anchor that designates this position. For example, anchors are $ and ^.
- **A character set**. These characters retain their literal meaning. And with no metacharacters, a character set is the simplest type of regular expression.

String manipulation and text search are the significant applications aimed at regular expression, and it is a part of a sequence or a string that matches a set of characters or a single character for a regular expression.

- Escaped "angle brackets" -- \<...\> -- mark word boundaries.

Since otherwise, they possess only their literal character and meaning, the angle brackets need to be escaped.

The word "the" matches " \<the\>" and not the words "*others*," "*there*," "*them*," etc. The only way to be sure that a particular regular expression works is to test it.

- The backlash -- \ -- their character gets interpreted as it escapes a unique character.

Instead of its regular expression meaning of end-of-line, a " \$\" reverts to its literal meaning of "$." Also, the literal meaning of "\' is a " \ \ ."

- Brackets – [...] – for a single regular expression to have a match, enclose a set of characters.

There is a match for common word patterns with the combination of sequences of bracketed characters. "there is a match between *yes, Yes, YES, yEs*, etc., and "[Yy][Ee][Ss]."

Another matches for any Social Security number are "[0-9][0-9][0-9][0-9][0-9][0-9][0-9][0-9][0-9].

Except for those in the range b to d, all characters match "[^*b-d*]." Inverting or negating ^ is a typical instance for the meaning of the following regular expression (in a different context, taking on a role similar to !).

Any digit or lowercase letter that matches "[a-z0-9]".

In the ranges of *k* to *y* and *b* to *P*, any of the characters that match "[B-Pk=y]."

In the range of *c* to *n*, any of the characters that match "[c-n]."

The characters x, y, or z match "[xyz]."

- The end of a regular expression matches the end of a line, which is the dollar sign -- $ --.

Matching blank lines is "^$."

At the end of the line, XXX matches "XXX$."

- The beginning of a line matches the caret --^-- and which negates the meaning of a set of characters in a regular expression depending on context sometimes.
- Except for a newline, any one character matches the dot --.—

Though, not *13* additional character missing, "13" matches *13 + at least one of any character, including space: 1133, 11333.*

- As well as *zero* instances, any number that has the repetition of the regular expression or character string matches the asterisk --*--.

"1133*" matches *11 + one or more 3's: 113, 1133, 1133333,* and so on.

- Extended regular expressions. Additional characters that the basic set have also. It is in *Perl*, *awk*, and *egrep* that they use it.
- One or more of a preceding regular expression matches the plus --+--. Though it does not match zero occurrences, it is the same role as in the * that it serves.
- Zero or one of the previous regular expression matches the question mark --?--. It is for matching single characters generally.
- Escaped "curly brackets" --\{\} – the previous regular expression to match is the indication of the number of the occurrences.

Because it is the literal character meaning that they only have otherwise, it is quite vital to escape the curly brackets. Technically, the fundamental regular expression arrangement does not correlate with this usage.

For the character in the 0 to 9 range, "[0-9]\{5\}" matches precisely five digits.

Note: as the non-POSIX compliant, classic `awk` version with a regular expression, curly brackets are not available. However, without being escaped, they have permission from the option `-re-interval` which gawk has. The versions that have no obligation from escaping the curly brackets are some **egrep** and **perl**.

- Parentheses – () – has in its enclosure a set of regular expressions. Using expr in substring extraction, with the following operator " | " they tend to be quite useful.
- The regular expression or the -- | -- the alternate character set matches it.

As do the GNU utilities, there is support for some version of *ex*, *ed*, and *sed* the lengthy regular expressions escaped version in the above description.

- Character Classes of POSIX. [:class:]

For the match of identifying characters range, this is an alternate method.

- [:xdigit:] matches hexadecimal digits. This is the same as 0-9A-Fa-f.
- [:upper:] matches uppercase characters of alphabets. As such, A-Z tends to be the same.
- [:space:] matches whitespace characters (horizontal and space tab).
- [:print:] (printable characters) in the scope of ASCII 32 – 126, it matches characters. Though adding the space character, this tends to be similar to the [:graph:] below.
- [:lower:] characters of the alphabet with a lowercase that matches. The a-z is quite the same as this.
- [:graph:] (graphic printable characters). Though excluding the space character, in the scale of ASCII 33 – 126, it matches characters. This is similar to [:print:] above.
- [:digit:] matches (decimal) digits. This is equivalent to 0-9.

- [:cntrl:] matches control characters.
- [:blank:] matches a tab or space.
- [:alpha:] matches alphabetic characters. This is equivalent to A-Za-z.
- [:alnum:] matches numeric or alphabetic characters. This is equivalent to A-Za-z0-9.

Conclusion

Thank you for making it through to the end of *LINUX Command-Line for Beginners: A Comprehensive Step-By-Step Starting Guide to Learn Linux from Scratch to Bash Scripting and Shell Programming*, let's hope it was informative and able to provide you with all of the tools you need to achieve your goals whatever they may be.

Chances are if you've made it to this point, it is because you want to know how you can navigate through the Linux operating system as well as having a clear grasp of the several command-lines and also the best ways of using them. You have made it to this point because you want to know all about many different pieces than Linux operating system comprises and also how you can install different distributions of Linux.

You will see that you can deal with types of installations for servers and also their roles. Reading through this book, you have learned how you can use Linux as a virtual machine inside another operating system, what dual booting is all about, and how you can boot Linux with the use of live CD/DVD.

In this book, you have read about Linux kernel and the operating systems, Linux directory structures, some of the fundamental Linux shell commands, how you can work with the disk, media, and data, and so much more. For you to get an understanding of how you can ideally use Linux and some of the associating programs, this book has shed enough light on essential terminals, editors, and shell.

Python Programming for Beginners

The Ultimate Crash Course to Learn Python Computer Language Faster and Easier
Introduction to Machine Learning and Artificial Intelligence

By Dylan Mach

© **Copyright 2019 by Dylan Mach - All rights reserved.**

The content contained within this book may not be reproduced, duplicated or transmitted without direct written permission from the author or the publisher.

Under no circumstances will any blame or legal responsibility be held against the publisher, or author, for any damages, reparation, or monetary loss due to the information contained within this book. Either directly or indirectly.

Legal Notice:

This book is copyright protected. This book is only for personal use. You cannot amend, distribute, sell, use, quote or paraphrase any part, or the content within this book, without the consent of the author or publisher.

Disclaimer Notice:

Please note the information contained within this document is for educational and entertainment purposes only. All effort has been executed to present accurate, up to date, and reliable, complete information. No warranties of any kind are declared or implied. Readers acknowledge that the author is not engaging in the rendering of legal, financial, medical or professional advice. The content within this book has been derived from various sources. Please consult a licensed professional before attempting any techniques outlined in this book.

By reading this document, the reader agrees that under no circumstances is the author responsible for any losses, direct or indirect, which are incurred as a result of the use of the information contained within this document, including, but not limited to, — errors, omissions, or inaccuracies.

Table of content

Introduction

Congratulations on purchasing *Python programming for beginners: The ultimate crash course to learn python computer language faster and easier* and thank you for doing so.

In this book, you will find a lot of really important and essential theories that will help you to get started into the Python programming language. Besides, you will find a lot of examples that will help you to understand in a more visual way the things that we have explained here.

In the following chapters you will find a short introduction to how programming languages started, who invented Python, who uses python nowadays, and all the information that is needed to learn Python from scratch such as variables, operators, data types, functions, loops, statements, exceptions, how to create classes, modules, a whole chapter about Object-Oriented Programming, also known as OOP, file handling of .txt, .PDF, .xlsx, and a lot of information that will make you a Python programmer.

We strongly recommend reading the codes here written, analyze them, understand them, and then try to do an example using each one of them in order to remember them easily. Because as you will see, there are tons of commands and statements that won't be easy to learn and remember if they are not used

There are plenty of books on this subject on the market, thanks again for choosing this one! Every effort was made to ensure it is full of as much useful information as possible, please enjoy!

Chapter 1: Introduction to Python

We can define programming as the process of designing, coding, debugging and maintaining the source code of a computer program, which means, that we say the steps to follow for the creation of the source code of computer programs.

The programming language, are all those rules or regulations, symbols and particular words used for the creation of a program, and with it, offer a solution to a particular problem. The best-known programming languages are: Basic (1964), C++ (1983), Python (1991), Java (1995), C# (2000), among others.

Programming is one of the stages for software development; programming specifies the structure and behavior of a program, verifying if it is working properly or not. Programming includes the specification of the algorithm defined as the sequence of steps and operations that the program must perform to solve a problem, for the algorithm to work, the program must be implemented in a compatible and correct language.

We could consider programming even easier than learning a new language because the programming language will be governed by a set of rules, which are, generally, always similar so you could say that it might be considered as a natural language.

In order to better understand the subject of programming, we could start with the beginnings of programming and how all this universe of languages and programs we know today began. We could start saying that programming began when the first computer was created in the fifteenth century, when a machine capable of doing basic operations and square roots appeared (Gottfried Wilhelm von Leibniz), although the one that actually served as a great influence for the creation of the first computer was the differential machine for calculating polynomials with the support of Lady Ada Countess (1815-1852), known as the first person who entered programming, and from whom comes the name of the programming language ADA, created by the DoD (Department of the United States), in the 1970s.

Initially, it was programmed in binary codes (bi=2), in other words, it consists of strings of 0s and 1s, which is the language directly understood by the computer, or what is known as machine language, a language considered fundamental for the commuter to be thus capable of interpreting the information supplied. Later the languages of high level appeared, using words in English, to give orders to follow, using intermediate processes between the language and the computer, this process can be a compiler or an interpreter.

The syntax of these programming languages is much simpler than our languages and they use a much smaller vocabulary and set of rules. In summary, we could say that programming is a set of sentences written in a programming language that tells the computer what tasks to perform and in what order, through a series of instructions that fully detail the process.

In the world of programming languages, we find interpreted languages, such as javascript, where a program called interpreter executes the sentences while reading the text file where they are written, which is why these programs are often also called scripts.

On the other hand, we have compiled languages such as Java, in this case, we must previously convert the text file to a "translation" through a program called compiler and the resulting file is the one that will finally run on the computer.

In this book we will speak specifically of the Python programming language, being this an interpreted language whose main and most important characteristic is the application of a syntax that favors the application of readable code. We could say that the interpreter is a type of program that executes a code directly, that is to say, it does not need to be compiled, and that is the case of our target language.

What is Python?

Python is one of the most important programming languages nowadays, being a general-purpose language, in this book you will have the language bases so that you can start with it. With this language, you can create a huge and variated amount of applications, because it allows you to create different kinds of applications since it doesn't have a defined purpose.

History of Python

This language was created by Guido Van Rossum in the early 1990s, at the Centre for Mathematics and Informatics (CWI, Netherlands), specifically in 1989, as Van Rossum himself explained in one of his interviews:

"In December 1989, I was looking for a hobby programming project to keep me busy during the Christmas weeks. My office would be closed and I would have nothing but my computer at home. I decided to write an interpreter for the new scripting language I had been coming up with recently: an ABC descendant that Unix/c hackers would like. I chose Python's name for the project, finding myself in a slightly irreverent state of mind (and being a big fan of Monty Python's Flying Circus)."

It began to be implemented in December 1989, and in February 1990 was released the first public version, version 0.9.0. Version 1.0 was released in January 1994, version 2.0 was released in October 2000 and version 3.0 was released on December 2008.

This programming language has as fundamental philosophy to have a syntax that favors a readable code, it is a high-level language that can be extended with C or C++, it has several programming environments that allow to edit programs, interact with the interpreter, develop projects, debug, among others and at the moment it is supported by a large community that facilitates its learning and that is producing a new progress in its already known new versions.

Python is a high-level programming language, interpreted and multipurpose, being currently one of the most used programming languages for software development. In recent years it has become a very valuable tool in the area of programming, this language is under a license of free software, under a license of Open Source or open-source approved by OSI (Open System Interconnect), so it is a program that can be used and distributed freely, either for personal or commercial use. The purpose of Python Software Foundation, "is to promote, protect and advance the Python programming language and to support and facilitate the growth of a diverse and international community of Python programmers".

The main advantage of an open and free technology is that it can be used without having to cover licensing costs. Free software is one of the most popular technological movements in the 21st century.

This language can be executed from any environment and distributed at the discretion of the user, modify if necessary, thus having a quick and easy basic tool for building programs.

To understand why we must learn python, it is necessary to understand the main characteristics of this language, that is why we will start talking about its main characteristics:

- It is a multiparadigm programming language, which means that we do not have to focus on a single way of programming, but we can do object-oriented programming, iterative programming, and functional programming, so we are not forced to focus on a single paradigm, hence its name of multiparadigm.

- It is a multiplatform language, which indicates that we can program in different environments or operating systems, such as Windows, Linux, etc..

- It is a very easy language to learn because it is simple and minimalist, and this is one of the main reasons why most people decide to have Python as their first programming language, because it has the simplest syntax to learn, it is an interpreted language, by this we mean that when executing a program, it will have the ability to execute itself taking instruction by instruction.

- It uses a dynamic typed, that can be explained in the following way, when we create a variable, and we store an initial type of data to it, the dynamic typed means that throughout the program this variable could change and store another value of another type of data, that later we will see this in detail.

- At the moment, we can also point out that this language occupies the position number four of the TIOBE index, which is an index that catalogs the languages according to their current popularity, being Java in first place, then in second place is the C language, in the third place is the C++ language and in the fourth Python, which indicates that it is a very popular and widely used language nowadays.

Now, knowing the characteristics of the program it is important to differentiate why we should learn Python and how it will serve us, what we can program with it, so well, being a general-purpose language, almost everything can be programmed with it: such as desktop applications with graphical interfaces and databases, web applications, games, custom applications, as a point of sale system for your business, for example, artificial intelligence, among others.

We will now talk about the development environment of this language, we can say that a development environment is a text editor in which we will be able to copy all the Python code, run our programs, do our tests, and so on. We will mention some of these editors, such as PyCharm, PyDev, Sublime Text 3, ATOM, VIM, as well as many others, in this book we will work with Visual Studio Code.

What can I do with Python?

As it is an easy to learn language, meaning it has a quite high learning curve, like many modern languages, as well as a very clean and simple syntax, as explained above, it is a very versatile language, because with it and the standard library we can write desktop applications and web applications. Python has excellent support for object-oriented programming (OOP), the only limitation for this language is your imagination. This programming language is built in such a way that there will always be a more optimal way to do things. This language is also used to work with artificial intelligence or robotics, where it is currently most used is for Big Data as it is a language that can handle a lot of data and complex operations.

In the area of video games:

The area of video games has its advantages and disadvantages, being Python an interpreted language, it is twice (or more) slower than a compiled language like Java, C++ or C#; you can do wonders of games in Python using libraries such as Pygame, SDL2 (Binding), OpenGL (binding), only that your game will not run as an executable made with C++ for example, instead it will run with the Python interpreter. But you will have an excellent language with a lot of support and documentation, and very few lines of code.

Finally, we can mention the scientific area, this is where Python shines. The syntax of Python and the bunch of libraries it gives you by default makes it perfect for scientific programming, plus in the Python community, there are huge libraries for mathematics and all that this entails.

Why should we use Python as a programming language?

Mainly we could say that we should use it because it is a very versatile language and general-purpose, this means that if your scope is not defined, you can create a huge number of applications using this language, suppose that your main goal is to create a web application, with Python you can do it, but probably tomorrow your interest will focus on scientific applications, because with Python you can also do it. In fact, the main development area of this language is the scientific area, if on the opposite you want to develop a low-level application, or you would like to use it in hardware because it is also possible to do it with this programming language, it is absolutely possible. That is why we talk about it being a versatile language since it does not have a rigorously defined scope.

Who uses Python today?

At the present time, this programming language is very commonly used, in addition, it has a wide range of uses, from the compilation and processing of data to the learning of a computer, which is why many of the important companies are currently working with this versatile programming language. We will mention some of these companies:

1. Google; it is a company that has handled this language from practically its beginning, in fact, its founders explained in one of their interviews that, "Python where we can, C++ where we must". This leads us to think that C++ is used for Google when memory control is imperative. So it is currently one of the company's official languages along with C++, Java and Go, which are the other three languages used. It is worth mentioning that Guido van Rossum himself worked in Google from 2005 to 2012, which indicates how important Python is for Google.

2. Facebook; in this company, Python is also part of this important social network, being in third place of language most used just behind C++, for example; in this company are handled more than five thousand confirmations of service and utilities such as infrastructure management, binary distribution, hardware images, and operational automation. As we have mentioned before, the ease of use of Python's libraries helps engineers to avoid having to maintain so many codes, making it easier to focus on brand optimization.

3. Spotify; one of the most important music companies today, is a large Python operator, due to how fast it is to write and encode on it. To provide suggestions and recommendations for all its users, Spotify relies heavily on a large volume of analysis and has Luigi, which is a Python module that synchronizes with Hadoop.

4. Netflix; this company uses python in a similar way to Spotify as it relies on this language to enhance its server-side analysis. Most of the engineers who work for this company are free to choose the language to work with, and most of them choose this language to encode.

5. Dropbox; this cloud-based storage system uses this language in its client's desktop. In 2012 Rossum joined this company on the condition that they would allow him to be just an engineer, not a leader or a manager, during his time at the company he helped to generate the ability to share data warehouses with other users within the Dropbox community.

6. Industrial Light and Magic (ILM) is a special effects center, founded by George Lucas himself in 1975, to create special effects for the well-known movies Star Wars. ILM selected Python 1.4, because it is much faster to integrate into their existing infrastructure, also, the easy Interoperability of

Python with C+ and C++ made easy for ILM to import Python into their patented lighting software.

In this way we can see how Python is in more and more places, using this language to wrap software components, expand graphic applications, among other skills, it has a wide range of code libraries and is more sensitive in development areas

How do I know which Python version should I use?

In Python, there are currently two versions that are incompatible between themselves, which causes a lot of confusion to any user who is starting to program or even any user who is starting in the same language. These versions are called Python 2.x which was released in 2000 and was updated until 2010, however, in 2008 was released version 3.x which is currently in full development of new versions and improvements in their commands.

But, do these versions contain the same tools?

Well, there is a big difference between each version of Python among which highlights that in Python 3.x the print sentence is taken into account as a function, so it is necessary to call it and enclose in parentheses what you want to print.

Unlike in the version 2.x which does not need parentheses to print.

When you are going to iterate a dictionary in Python version 2.x, the key-value elements are used through the items() and iteritems() methods. In the current version of Python 3.x, this operation is done only through the items(), keys() and values() methods and when using the iteritems() method we will obtain an exception of the AttributeError type.

There is also a change in the input function, which in the Python 2.x version takes the data without converting the variable type. In this version, if we enter an integer variable, its entry will be of the "int" type and if we want it to be treated as a string we would have to call the function "raw_input" since this will be in charge of converting "int" data to string.

In the Python 3.x version, this takes a big step forward since the "raw_input" function is suppressed and any conversion would be easily done through the input() function.

Now that I know which version to use, how can I install Python according to my operating system?

The Python programming language is included by default in the Mac OS and Linux operating systems, the only thing to do is to update according to the version you have, however, for Windows users, the program must be installed since it is not included in the system.

Install Python on Windows

Go to https://www.python.org/downloads/

Choose the version of your preference to install: 2.x and 3.x. It is always recommended for new users to use the latest version of Python (3.x), this facilitates understanding thanks to its simplified tools. However, if you are using a recycled code, it is recommended to use the version in which it was written.

Once the download is finished, run the program.

If you are a new user, it is recommended to install Python with its default settings. If you are a language experienced user, you can do the custom installation.

Verify that the program and its interpreter work correctly.

Install or upgrade Python for Mac OS

Python comes by default in OS X with version 2.7. If you need to upgrade your version to 3.x just follow these steps:

Enter python.org/downloads on your computer, the link will automatically detect the operating system you have and it will show you the files compatible with the computer to start the download.

Click on the PKG file to start its installation and if you are a new user.

Start the Python program by typing "Python3" in order to start the interface of this new version.

Installing or Upgrading Python For Linux

In almost all Linux distributions Python is previously installed by default, so it is not necessarily needed to install but rather update, the only detail is that for a policy issue of installation the vast majority comes with Python 2.x and not with Python 3.x, as should be, especially if we consider that most modern applications require or recommend version 3.x to compile.

To upgrade Python, just follow these steps:

Check the Python version you have, since the Linux Operating System is included with the program, however, its version may vary.

On the Linux terminal type "sudoapt-get install Python".

Then in the same terminal type "sudo yum install Python".

Enter as a root user by typing "pacman-S python".

Finally, start the program and check that it works correctly so you can start programming.

Learning to use Python

Once Python is downloaded, you will need a code editor that allows you to interpret and write code for programs. There is a great variety of editors, this depends and goes according to the preference and level of experience of the user with the programming since it will be your ally while programming.

Among the best-known editors are:

Visual Studio Code: It is a multi-platform source code editor with a dark interface; it has an optimized user interface. This editor has multiple tools and even allows real-time updates of our code while compiling. You do not need a complete IDE and it is possible to change the appearance of your interface through the themes it brings.

Visual Studio Code supports a wide variety of languages, including Python, Php, Java, C++, Ruby, Go, C, SQL, JavaScript, Batch, and Objective-C.

Sublime text: This is a multiplatform editor with a dark interface, which allows to execute a great variety of documents in multiple tabs and offers a full-screen mode, thus facilitating the user's visual space in the computer. This has a panel that allows you to move through the code quickly and easily. Sublime text is capable of interpreting a wide variety of programming languages such as Python, CSS, C++, HTML, Matlab, R, SQL, C, Php) and has autosave, another fact and advantage of this editor is that it allows running files in Python with just a shortcut on the keyboard; Ctrl+B.

Geany: This is a multiplatform code editor of the Linux operating system, which is ideal for application development and even software development for this operating system and also that it is possible to operate on operating systems such as Windows, Mac OS or any other system with GTK library support. In addition, this editor is distinguished for being fast and lightweight, is completely independent and supports languages such as HTML, C++, JAVA, PHP, PYTHON, and C.

Wing: This is another paid integrated development environment for Python, it is owned by the company Wingware. It was created mainly for professional developers. It offers a great set of tools and features necessary for Python programming, it is compatible with Windows, OS X, and Linux and works with Python 3.x versions. Wing has a free basic version, a personal edition and a professional edition which can be considered very powerful when creating a program.

Komodo Edit: This is an open-source editor oriented to dynamic languages including Python, JavaScript, HTML, CSS, Perl, NodeJS. Komodo is considered one of the most popular code editors for applications today and also has a premium package that includes a number of useful tools, such as allowing writing codes and collaborating in the development of other codes in real-time, exploring databases, removing bugs. It is mostly focused on small project developers.

Ninja IDE: This is a text editor for development, which will only allow us to create projects in Python and at the same time run them in order to correct any errors that may occur at any moment.

Python's Keywords:

It is well known that in every programming language there is a series of words and commands which are found in a reserved way and can not be used for anything other than to fulfill its function. In Python there is also has a set of words, these are called: reserved words or keywords, and are nothing more than a set of words in which each element contains a special meaning and is an indispensable part of the syntax of its language for the correct development of the code.

These words must be written exactly as shown in the following table, which will contain some of the reserved words of the language. If this is not done, the program will not be able to recognize them and can generate a type of exception called: NameError, this is because Python does not distinguish between upper and lower case or as it is formally known: case sensitive.

If we write false, the Python interpreter will not be able to understand that we are referring to the False operator and will throw us an error because this is not defined.

The following table will show the set of keywords for the Python 3.x version (version with which we are going to work in the next programs), which have defined approximately 33 reserved words; these same ones form the nucleus of the syntax of this programming language.

"and"	"def"	"finally"	"in"	"or"	"while"
"as"	"del"	"for"	"is"	"pass"	"with"
"assert"	"elif"	"from"	"lambda"	"raise"	"yield"
"break"	"else"	"global"	"None"	"return"	
"class"	"except"	"if"	"nonlocal"	"True"	
"continue"	"False"	"import"	"not"	"try"	

Of this group, there are a certain number of words which are considered " essential ", these could be the ones we are going to use the most and we will explain them in-depth in the next chapters.

True & False: These expressions are those whose values are thrown to us by the program as a result of evaluating logical expressions.

and & or: These expressions are those that we use as connectors for the logical expressions (True & False), in order to be able to create much more complex expressions.

if, elif & else: These expressions are those which are used to build blocks of conditions, in order to make certain decisions within the same programs.

For & while: These expressions are used to build loops or formally: repetitive blocks.

Def & return: These expressions are those that represent instructions, which will be used to define our own functions. In other words: these expressions represent a series of instructions that will be in charge of carrying out a certain task as indicated.

Import & from: These expressions are those used to add additional functionalities.

If you are using a code that has been written in Python 2.x version or you simply want to start in this version, we can see that unlike Python 3.x version, this version has only 31 reserved words or keywords.

"and"	"def"	"finally"	"in"	"print"	"yield"
"as"	"del"	"for"	"is"	"raise"	
"assert"	"elif"	"from"	"lambda"	"return"	
"break"	"else"	"global"	"not"	"try"	
"class"	"except"	"if"	"or"	"while"	
"continue"	"exec"	"import"	"pass"	"with"	

What are the differences in keywords between Python 2.x and Python 3.x?

Below, we will mention those important differences that cannot be noticed at first sight:

- Python 3.x incorporates the words "True", "False" and "None".

- In Python 2.x the words "exec" and "print" that were part of the keywords, become integrated functions in Python 3.x with the syntax exec() and print().

How can I find these words?

In Python, there is a module whose name is known as keyword module of the standard library, this is responsible for exporting a list called: kwlist. which contains all the keywords that are reserved in our programming language, Python.

Another easier way to consult these keywords is through the help() command, this is just a function that comes integrated and facilitates us to consult information, documentation and get a clearer help on the components of our program.

If in any given situation you need to quickly consult the operation or meaning of a particular keyword (only of the Python programming language), you can do it through the command help(), once introduced this, you must write the keyword to consult and immediately will show us on screen all the information of the word requested.

Python syntax and its importance

Now we will talk about the most important thing and it will be what will allow us to advance in our code and in programming in general: The syntax; we know very well that Python is an interpreted programming language, but what does this really mean?

Our Python programming language works through tabulations, this is informally known as indentation or spaces. This means that, at the moment of executing a program, it is going to follow an order of interpretation, which works through the tab key on our keyboard which is just the key containing arrows located above Caps Lock, these tabs work in each loop or conditional sentence.

When we have a correct indentation we can avoid the use of keys and brackets and we can even avoid some reserved words to start and end a program that marks a block of code. This allows the program to have better use and operation.

Having a good indentation also helps us to make our code look uniform in order to facilitate reading and provide comfort to any third party who reads it, and even to ourselves, because we can locate an error effectively and quickly.

It is important to emphasize that the first line of the code should never be indented, the indentation will always go after this and with 4 boxes of space.

Physical and logical lines: A program in Python is composed of a set of logical lines, they are formed by a certain amount of physical lines.

But... What are physical lines?

Physical lines are those lines that are used to enumerate our code editor, or formally can be described as a sequence of characters which end when entering the end-of-line character "\n".

And what are logical lines?

Logical lines are those that go with Python syntax logic components and their end is determined by the NEWLINE token which determines the end of each line and starts another.

These physical lines have the ability to be united through an action called "implicit union of lines" to form a single logical line, using characters such as parentheses (), square brackets [] and keys {}.

If we start a logical line with the start characters such as "(", "[", "{" it will extend through all the necessary logical lines until it ends with its closing symbol ")", "[", "{".

There are two types of statements in Python:

Simple statements: These types of statements are those that must be completed in a single logical line. For example:

Print objects in the program: print()

Generate exceptions: raise EndSearch (location)

Access Attributes: from sys import stdin

Access modules: import sys

Execute functions through expressions: log.write()

Compound statements: These types of statements are those that must begin with the compound statement clause, followed by the contained statement on the next line. This must be correctly indented since it will be part of the body of our code. It will always start with a keyword and end with a colon ":".

An example of compound sentences is sequence and iteration for, else, else, if, elif, loops while, and else.

Make comments in the code: A comment in Python refers to a set of characters which are not executable, these are made in a text line of our program. The comment is represented with the numeral character (#). At the moment of programming, the comments can be very useful to be able to explain in detail each action carried out in a program code to people outside the code, or even for ourselves.

Our first program: Hello world

Once we have installed the code editor of our preference and already knowing a little about the Python programming language syntax, we can proceed to write our first program: Hello world.

If you already have experience in programming is common to ask yourself, "Why is "Hello World" always the first program to enter any programming language? Well, the simple phrase Hello World is characterized by being an extremely simple code, especially at the time of running and can serve as a test to ensure that we have installed our program well and its interpreter. In this way, when working with heavy programs we are going to be sure that everything will work correctly.

From now on all the examples will be based on version 3.x for better understanding.

The syntax that we are going to use for this code will be: print("Hello World");

Running a program on Linux

1. Create a directory called projects on your primary user's desktop

2. Create a plain text file with the name: Helloworld.py

3. Type the syntax of your code

4. Run the following command: Home/projects/Helloworld.py.

5. Once this is done, your code should be displayed as indicated.

To run in windows:

1. Create a directory called projects in unit C: \

2. Within this directory, we'll need to create a plain text file

3. Write the code syntax

4. Save the file as Helloworld.py (the name may vary according to your preference)

5. Run from the MS-DOS console: C:Python27\Python C:\Projects\Helloworld.py, or also from the same program Visual Studio, you can do F5.

6. Once this is done, your code should be shown on screen as indicated.

Running a program on Mac OsX

1. Click on File in a new browser window.

2. Create a folder with the name of your preference, in which you will save future projects.

3. Within this folder, we will need to create a new folder called Projects (all programs will be stored here).

4. Click on Applications and then on TextEdit.

5. Select Plain Text.

6. Type the syntax of the program.

7. Click on "save as" from the menu file in TextEdit.

8. Save the file as: Helloworld.py (or the name of your preference) and select the folder already mentioned.

9. Select Applications, then utilities and terminal.

10. Select the folder in which you saved your program.

11. Run cd of the folder.

12. Execute ls and it should show on screen the file Helloworld.py

13. Type the following command: Helloworld.py

Once this is done, your code should be displayed as indicated

Chapter 2: Variables

Flow control

What are flow diagrams?

They are tools that are used for any type of programming language, which are used to represent or create the structure of the program or algorithm.

The flow diagrams or also called flowchart, are a way to graphically represent an algorithm (the steps that are executed in the program), facilitating its interpretation to a person.

The creation of the structure of the algorithm or program can be considered the first part of the development of the algorithm and the preparation for the most important step that is coding.

At the time of elaborating a program, it is advisable to make a flowchart so that any person can understand in a simple way the function of the algorithm. Currently, there are a variety of software and online tools that facilitate the elaboration of these diagrams.

Main figures and meaning:

	Start / end: Indicates the starting or ending of the diagram
	Input / Output of data: These are data which are assigned to the input and output variables at the beginning and ending of our code.
	Process: This is what executes the order of the operation
	Decision: Indicates a position in the flowchart, this is used for logical expressions. In this case, the sequence is going to split in two cases, a positive and a negative one. This is also used to apply conditionals
	Document: This is used generally to make a document
	Inspection: This is used for some cases where an inspection is required.

| 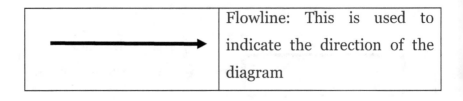 | Flowline: This is used to indicate the direction of the diagram |

For example:

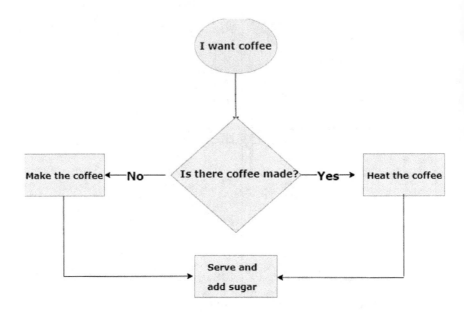

Variables

What are the variables in Python?

It is quite sure that we have always heard the concept of variable in mathematics since these are defined as an unknown symbol represented by letters (x, y, z, i, n) which (mostly) store a numerical value.

In this case, when we talk about variables in programming, these represent a space reserved in the memory of our program or computer that can be modified and used multiple times. These variables have a very similar representation and meaning; since they represent a box capable of storing values. Unlike mathematical variables, these can store complex words such as cities, names, passes, simple letters, and ages.

In Python, a variable can be interpreted as a "label" to the data information stored box, and these data can be understood as objects. Python is also able to distinguish between upper and lower case letters (as we previously mentioned this is known as case sensitive), which means that it will not be the same to call a variable Song to a variable called song.

We cannot forget that being Python a programming language that is object-oriented, the data structure of our programs will be based on these same, therefore, the label we put to the variables cannot match the names of the commands or otherwise it will throw us an error.

Declare variables in Python

Python has the advantage of being a dynamic programming language; this means that it is not necessary to specify the type of data with which we will work since its interpreter is able to infer the type of data to use. Unlike C++ that, to declare a variable, it is necessary and obligatory to specify the type of data with which the variable will be stored in the memory so that its compiler can be able to interpret it.

For example:

As we can see, Python uses the symbol "=" to assign the values to the variable, once this is done the variable starts with this value, since there is no possible way to declare a variable without any initial value.

```
variable.py ●
 ▷ ...          ▷ variable.py ▷ ...
 1    x= 2
 2    X= 4
 3
 4
```

We can observe in this example the declaration of two variables of name x with different values, this is totally valid since as we can observe, a variable is written in small letters and another variable is written in capital letters.

It is important to keep in mind that in Python there are operations that, when defined, are not allowed between types (classes) that are not compatible, so that when each data is identified it becomes an inherited object to the type of data to which it belongs.

To be able to declare a variable it is necessary for it to go from left to right, otherwise, it will result in a syntax error.

```
variable.py ●
          ▷  variable.py
   1    2 = x
   2    4 = X
   3
   4    SyntaxError: can't assign to literal
```

It is essential that variable names begin with a letter or underscore (the rest of the name can contain letters, numbers, and underscores).

```
variable.py ●
          ▷  variable.py ▷ ...
   1    X= 2 # Valid #
   2    _X= 4 #Valid#
   3
   4    2x = 4 #Error, starts with numeral data #

        SyntaxError: invalid syntax

        !x = False # Error, starts with symbol #
        SyntaxError: invalid syntax
```

It is also possible to assign multiple values to multiple variables on the same line, as long as there are the same number of arguments on both the left and right.

```
          ▷  variable.py ▷ ...
   1    a, b, c= 2, 4, 6
   2
```

Data Types

- Integers: Integer data in Python can identify integers of either decimal, binary, hexadecimal, or octal type.

There are two ways to declare a variable as integer: An int is placed prior to the variable name as follows:

```
variable.py ×
     ▶  variable.py
  1    int Number = 4
  2
```

The other way is the most common, in which we only write the name of the variable to be declared.

```
variable.py ●
     ▶  variable.py ▶ ...
  1    Number = 4
  2
```

- Float: The data of the type float are in charge of covering all the set of real numbers ex: 3.14, 21, -85.6. When we perform an operation with float type data, it will not always give us a result with an exact number, many times it can be an approximation and its declaration is very similar to the declaration of variables of the integer type.

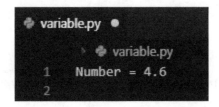

```
 variable.py
         variable.py
1    Number = 4.6
2
```

- Complex: The data of the complex type refer to the set of operations with complex numbers, these are expressed as data of the type float separated by the operand symbol, the first number is going to present to the real number and its imaginary component is going to be identified being accompanied by a letter j. At the moment of declaring a variable of the complex type it must be declared in the following way:

```
 variable.py
        variable.py ▶ ...
1    vari = complex(4+14j)
2    print(vari)
3
```

- String: Data of the string type refers to a sequence or string of characters that are enclosed in apostrophes or quotation marks.

String types:

\": double quotation mark.

\': single quotation mark.

185

\n: Line break.

\t: Tab horizontally.

Example:

```
variable.py
    variable.py ▸ ...
1   string= "Hello world"
2   string2= "This is my String example"
3   print(string)
4   print(string2)
```

- Bool: Boolean data consists of only two (2) digits, which evaluate logical expressions. This is very important for future chapters because it will allow us to understand conditionals or cycles.

  If a logical expression is true, its numerical value will be 1.

  If a logical expression is false, its numerical value will be 0.

- Lists: List type data allows the program to store within it, certain items of any different data type, as well as being able to have repeated items. These same are written with curly brackets.

```
variable.py  ●

            variable.py  ▸ …
1    a = 2
2    b = 4
3    string = "Hello people"
4    bool= True
5
6    list=[a, b, string, bool, 3, False, "good luck"]
7
8    print(list)
```

- Tuples: Tuples type data are able to store several items within it, this type of data can be similar to lists but differs in the following things: Their declaration is made with a parenthesis (), unlike the lists that are declared with square brackets []; when we declare Tuples, these same are immutable, unlike the lists that when we declare them, can be changed, and finally because they are immutable, their search for data is much more effective than in a list.

  His statement is as follows:

```
variable.py  ●

         ▸  variable.py  ▸ …
1    a = 2
2    b = 4
3    string = "Tuple"
4    bool= True
5
6    Tup=(a, b, string, bool)
7
8    print(Tup)
```

187

- Set: This type of data in Python is based on a data structure, which can consist of multiple elements whose order in the set is not defined. Sets are able to add, remove and iterate elements of a set, as well as perform common operations such as differentiate, verify if an element belongs to the set, differentiate and intersect.

To define a set we only need to name the function set (). If it has a list, a tuple or a string, it will return a compound of the elements. Example:

```
variable.py ×
        ▸ variable.py ▸ ...
1    A = {5, 3, 2}
2    A = set('PYTHON')
3    print(A)
```

- Dictionaries: This type of data is defined as a structure that has certain special characteristics that allow us to store any integer value, list, string, and even functions. Dictionaries allow us to identify each element by a key.

It is important to keep in mind that when working with dictionaries the 'keys' cannot be repeated data, likewise, it is not possible to access the keys through their associated value.

It is also important to know that these do not meet a specific order, but that this type of data is guided by the keys.

In order to define a dictionary, we enclose with curly brackets {} the list of values to be entered. Each key pair is separated with commas and the key together with the value is separated by a colon. For example:

```
variable.py
     variable.py
1    user = {'name' : 'John', 'Age' : 20, 'Knowledge': ['Python progamming','C++ programming','JavaScript']}
2
3    print (user['name'])
4    print (user['Age'])
5    print (user['Knowledge'])
```

That will print:

```
John
20
['Python progamming', 'C++ programming', 'JavaScript']
```

Here we can see that we have created the dictionary and also the program shows us that we have accessed each key separately.

Dictionary methods:

get(): This method receives a key as a parameter and returns its value. If it doesn't find a value, it returns an object of type none. For example:

```
variable.py
    variable.py ▸ ...
1    user={'name' : 'John', 'age' : 20, 'knowledge': ['Python programming','C++ programming','JavaScript'] }
2    print(user.get('name'))
3
```

In this case, it will return the value name, which in this case will be John.

Item(): This type of method is in charge of returning a list of tuples, in which each one is composed of two elements in which the first element will be the key and the second element will be its value. For example:

```
variable.py  ×
    variable.py ▸ ...
1    user={'name' : 'John', 'age' : 20, 'knowledge': ['Python programming','C++ programming','JavaScript'] }
2    print(user.items())
```

Keys(): This type of method only returns the keys of our dictionary. Example:

```
variable.py  ×
    variable.py ▸ ...
1    user={'name' : 'John', 'age' : 20, 'knowledge': ['Python programming','C++ programming','JavaScript'] }
2    print(user.keys())
```

Values(): This type of method only returns the values of their respective keys from our dictionary.

```
variable.py ×
        variable.py ▸ ...
  1   user={'name' : 'John', 'age' : 20, 'knowledge': ['Python programming','C++ programming','JavaScript'] }
  2   print(user.values())
```

Clear(): This method eliminates all the items and leaves our dictionary empty. For example:

```
variable.py ×
        variable.py ▸ ...
  1   user={'name' : 'John', 'age' : 20, 'knowledge': ['Python programming','C++ programming','JavaScript'] }
  2   print(user.clear())
```

Copy(): This method returns a copy of the original dictionary. For example:

```
variable.py ×
        variable.py ▸ ...
  1   user={'name' : 'John', 'age' : 20, 'knowledge': ['Python programming','C++ programming','JavaScript'] }
  2   print(user.copy())
```

Redeclaring variables in Python:

A great advantage that Python has is its ability to allow redeclaring variables in a simple way, from changing their value to changing the type of variable without complications. For example:

```
variable.py ●

        ▸  variable.py ▸ ...
1    a=4
2    print(a)
3    a=8
4    print(a)
5    a=True
6    print(a)
7    a= "Julia"
8    print(a)
9
```

In the last example, we can observe that the first declaration of the variable "a" is assigned the value 4, which is an integer, then the variable is redeclared with the value 8, therefore, at that time the variable is integer, then we have redeclared the variable again and we have converted it to a Boolean value, since we have assigned it the value True. Finally, we have assigned to the variable a string which we can see as a name "Julia" so at that time the variable is of string type.

Concatenate strings

To concatenate character strings we will only need to use the addition operand (+). It is important to note that you must specifically and explicitly mark the place where we want to leave the space blank.

```
variable.py ●

        ▷  variable.py ▷ ...
1    a= "Hello world"
2    b=" this is an example"
3    c= a + b
4    print(c)
```

As we can see in the last example, the variable "a" was created, which contained the value "Hello world", then the variable "b" was created, which contained the value "this is an example" and later the final variable "c" was created, this last one was in charge of carrying out the concatenation of "a" and "b".

The concatenation of variables can also be done with integer and boolean values, but to do this you must convert these variables into strings beforehand. How do you do this? Well, it's very simple, we do it calling the function str(). For example:

```
variable.py ✕

     variable.py ▸ ...
1    string= "class of "
2    date= 2019
3    date=str(date)
4    final=string + date
5    print(final)
```

As we could see in the example, we have created a string variable that contains the value "class of ", and then the integer type date variable is created and contains the value "2019". Then we redeclare our variable date to string type with the function str().

Another very common example is concatenating lists, this we do through the function extend(), for example:

```
variable.py ●

     variable.py ▸ ...
1    lunch = ["Sanwich", "pizza", "Burger", "meat"]
2    snack = ["ice cream", "cookie", "brownie", "cake"]
3    lunch.extend(snack)
4    print(lunch)
```

We can see in the previous example that a list has been created with some lunch options; then another list has been created with some snack options and finally, the command lunch.extend(snack) is created concatenating list number 1 with list number 2.

Global Variables

Global variables are those used throughout the program; once declared, they may be used as a main function or any other type of function.

This type of variable can be modified in any part of the program, this could seem an advantage, but it could also cause confusion both for the programmer or another external person who is going to read the program. Another point that could be considered negative with global variables is that they can take up more space than common ones because they cannot be destroyed at the end of running the function, on the other hand, this one does not allow the code to be reusable; this makes Python programming language one of the most attractive.

In general terms, it is considered a bad practice to work with global variables, but it is never too much to have complete knowledge. Next, we will see how to declare a global variable.

For this it is necessary to use the global command:

```
  variable.py  ●
            variable.py ▷ ...
1     global var
2     var = 2019
3     print(var)
```

As we could see in the last example, calling or declaring a global variable is not very complicated. We could say that it is similar to what we have seen to declare variables; the only difference is that from now on the variable "var" is going to have a global character so that any function is going to be able to access it in a simple way.

Local variables

Local variables are those that are only used in one function and are deleted from memory when their execution is completed. Unlike global variables, local variables allow us to save quantities of lines of codes, making modular programming much more agile and easy, thus allowing the reuse of the code, which makes Python one of the most striking programming languages.

The main advantage of using local variables in a Python program is that it facilitates the reading of the code, making it simple to understand; global variables allow any error to be fixed more effectively and easily. Having reduced lines of code, it is very unlikely that confusion will be generated at the time of interpreting it.

It is considered a good practice to use local variables at the moment of programming since nowadays it is intended to obtain much simpler codes to interpret by users who do not have so much experience in programming.

To better understand this, we will make an example that explains in a clear way the use of these variables at the moment of programming.

Example: We are going to create a problem in which it must be responsible for taking the following data from a person:

1. Name and Lastname

2. Age

3. Country of origin

```
variable.py ×
    variable.py ▸ ...
1   full_name = input("Full name: ")
2   age = input("Age: ")
3   country_origin = input("country of origin: ")
4   print("Full name"+full_name + "\n" + "Age"+ age + "\n"+"Country of origin" + country_origin)
5
```

We can observe that the syntax focuses more than everything on the input() command, what does this mean? This is only the function that allows a user-program interaction to be possible. In this way, the variables "full_name", "age" and "country_origin" will have the value that the user introduces at the moment to the console.

```
Full name: Python programmer
Age: 100
country of origin: Worldwide
```

Chapter 3: Operators

Operators are mathematical symbols that carry out a specific operation between operands, operators can receive variable operands. Operands are those arguments that operators receive in order to perform their functions. So we can conclude that operators are those special symbols that are capable of performing logical and arithmetic operations.

Types of operators:

- Logic operators.

- Arithmetic operators.

- Comparison operators.

- Assignment operators.

- Special operators.

- Logical or conditional operators: This type of operators are those that are commonly used to group, deny and exclude some expressions of our code.

1. Operator not: This type of operator is the one in charge of negating or returning a value opposite to the Boolean value.

not True=False.

not False=True.

2. Operator Or: This type of operator is the one that evaluates the values on the right side and the values on the left side in order to finally return a true value if at least one condition is met.

False or True = True

True or false = True

True or True = True

False or False = False

3. Operator And: This type of operator is responsible for assessing whether the conditions between the value on the left side and the value on the right side are met correctly:

True and False = False

True and True = True

False and True = False

False and False = False

- Comparison operators: These types of operators are those that we use to compare (as its name says) some values stored in the program so that later this at the time of compiling we can return a value of the True / False type as a result of fulfilling a condition.

1. Operator !=: This type of operator is in charge of evaluating if these stored values are different and depending on the result of the analysis, this will give us a True/False. E.g.

20!=20 The result is going to be False

14!= 15 The result will be True

2. Operator ==: This type of operator is in charge of evaluating if these values are the same for different types of data and

depending on the result obtained in its analysis, its result will give us a True/False. E.g.

19 = = 19 The result will be True

10 = = 5 The result will be False

3. Operator >: This type of operator is in charge of evaluating whether the value entered on the left side has a position greater than that of the value positioned on the right side. E.g.

30>25 The result will be True

9> 28 The result will be False

4. Operator <: This type of operator is the one that will evaluate if the value entered on the left side has a lower position than the value positioned on the right side. E.g.

26<9 Result will be False

14 < 22 The result will be True

5. Operator >=: This type of operator is in charge of evaluating whether the value entered on the left side has a position greater than or equal to that of the value positioned on the right side. E.g.

20> 14 The result will be True

10 > 26 The result will be False

10 >= 10 The Result will be True

6. Operator <=: This type of operator is the one that will evaluate if the value entered on the left side has a position less than or equal to the value positioned on the right side. E.g.

20 < 11 The result will be False

16 < 25 The result will be True

15 <= 15 The result will be True

- Assignment operators: These types of operators are those that are used in the program to assign (as its name says) a value to a variable, in this case, these operators will be followed by a symbol of equality (=)

1. Operator Equality (=): This type of operator is considered the main one and will always be positioned on the left side of the variable. E.g.

> A= 10 → The value of A will be 10

2. Operator Sum - equality (+=) This type of operator is responsible for adding to the variable on the left side, with the value located on the right side. E.g.

> A= 10; A += 8 → A= 18

It would be equivalent to expressing: A=10; A + 8 → A=18

3. Operator subtracts - equality (-=) This type of operator is the one that subtracts from the variable on the left side, with the value located on the right side. E.g.

> A= 10; A -= 8→ A= 2

It would be equivalent to expressing: A=10; A - 8 → A= 2

4. Operator Rest - equality (%=) This type of operator is responsible for returning the rest of the division on the left side, to the value located on the right side.

>A= 10; A %= 8 → A = 2

It would be equivalent to expressing A= 10; A % 8 → A= 2

5. Integer Operator - equality (//) This type of operator is responsible for calculating the integer division of the variable on the left side, with the value located on the right side.

> A= 10; A //= 8 → A= 1

It would be equivalent to expressing A= 10; A // 8 → A= 1

6. Operator Product - equality (*=) This type of operator is responsible for multiplying the variable on the left side, with the value located on the right side. E.g.

> A= 10; A *= 8 → A = 80

It would be equivalent to expressing: A=10; A * 8 → A= 80

7. Operator Division - equality (/=) This type of operator is in charge of dividing the variable on the left side, with the value located on the right side. E.g.

>A= 10; A /= 8 → A= 1,25

It would be equivalent to expressing A= 10; A * 8 → A= 1,25

8. Exponent Operator - equality (**=) This type of operator is responsible for calculating the exponent of the variable on the left side, with the value located on the right side. E.g.

>A= 10; A **= 8 → A = 100000000

It would be equivalent to expressing A= 10; A ** 8 → A= 100000000

- Special Operators: These types of operators are commonly used in program loops, to check for repeated variables and even to know if an element is stored within others.

1. Operator In: This operator will return a 'True' if an element is stored inside another. E.g.

A= [80, 40] 80 in A

The result that is going to return will be of the true type because the value 80 is positioned in A

2. Operator Is: This type of operator will return a True if its values stored in the variables are the same. E.g.

X= 80; Y= 80. → X is Y

The result to be returned will be of the True type because both variables contain the same stored value.

3. Operator Not in: This type of operator will return a True if an element is not stored inside another element. E.g.

A= [80, 40] 40 not in A.
The result that is going to return will be of the False type because the value 40 if it is positioned in A.

4. Operator Not is: This type of operator will return a True if the values stored in the variables are not equal. E.g.

X= 80; Y=40. → X not is Y

The result that is going to return will be of the True type because both variables contain stored different values, therefore, they are different.

- Arithmetic Operators: These types of operators are those used to perform simple mathematical operations.

1. Sum Operator (+): This type of operator will add values of the numerical type. E.g.

$$40 + 40 = 80$$

2. Operator subtracts (-): This type of operator will subtract values from the numerical type. E.g.

$$40 - 40 = 0$$

3. Operator multiplication (*): This type of operator will multiply numerical values. E.g.

$$40 * 40 = 1600$$

4. Operator division (/): This type of operator will be responsible for dividing numerical type values. E.g.

$$10 / 2 = 5$$

5. Exponent operator (**): This type of operator will calculate the exponent of a stored value between values with numerical data type. E.g.

$$4^{**} 2 = 16$$

6. Integer Division Operator (//): This type of operator is responsible for calculating the integer division of a stored value with numeric data type in which only the integer part will return. E.g.

$5 // 2 = 2$

Note: It is important to note that, when working with two operands of the integer type, the program will assume that you want the variable to yield a result of the integer type. E.g.

If we operate A= $7 // 2$ = Our result will be 3.

If you want to get the decimals as in the first example, just add at least one decimal value to either of the two operands. E.g.

$G = 7.0 / 2 = 3.5$

7. Operator Module: This type of operator is responsible for returning the rest of the division between the two operands. Ex,=.

$7 \% 2 = 1$. The division module is 1

The order of precedence or priority of arithmetic operators is as follows:

1. Exponent (**)

2. Multiplication (*), Division (/), Whole Division (//), Module (%)

In line 2 we can see that the rest of the operators are grouped together, this means that they all have the same order of priority, but at the time of operating they will be resolved by that order of precedence.
Example:
When operating: 8*10/2

This means that the operation is to be carried out as follows: 8*10= 80 / 2 = 40. The result of our operation is 40.

On the other hand, this order of precedence can be manipulated by using parentheses ().

Example:

When operating 80*(10/2)

This means that the operation is to be carried out as follows: 10/2= 5 * 4 = 20.
Let's make two small examples to work with operators, let's calculate the area of a rectangle and the other is to see if the key is correct.

First example, area of the rectangle:

```
operators.py ✕

1    b=int(input("Please enter the base: "))
2    h=int(input("Please enter the height: "))
3    print("The area is "+str(b*h))
4
```

In this example, the first thing we do is to declare the variables, the first is variable b, which is related to the base, which goes through several stages, but we put it in a single line to save space.

To explain it better, the first thing we can observe is that there is an input in the declaration of both b and h, which is an input type, so that it is going to be saved as a string, for this reason, we can also observe the int function, which will turn that string into an integer, to be able to do operations on them. Do you know why is that?

Because it is impossible to add two strings, since it is very different to add 1 + 1 than "1" + "1", because the first is a sum of integers, and its result will be equal to 2, but the second we do not know, because it is a sum of ASCII characters. And well, as you can see, the same thing is done with the variable h, therefore, b and h are two integers entered by the user.

The next action is to print in screen the following string "The area is" concatenated with the string related to the multiplication of the base and the height, because it is not possible to concatenate a string with an integer, for this reason, the function str() is used.

As you can see, this is a very basic example, and here comes a question, what happens if you enter a negative value? If, for example, you enter -5 and 2, the value returned will be -10, and this is a big mistake since there are no negative areas, therefore, it is an error that our program has. The errors can be solved by using conditionals, or also with the handling of exceptions since they will take into account these cases.

Second example, key verification:

```
operators.py

1    password="12345"
2    passuser=input("Please enter the password here: ")
3    print("User "+str(password==passuser))
4
```

The first thing is that we define the password variable as a string "12345", then, the passuser variable is declared, which is related to the input function, it will show on the screen "Please enter the password here: ", the same will make in passuser is a string.

Finally, it will be printed in screen if the key is correct or not, for it, will be printed in screen "User" and this one will concatenate with the result of comparing if password is strictly equal to passuser, but in order for this to be concatenated, it will be necessary to convert this comparison into a string, because it is necessary to delimit that when some comparison is made, the return is a boolean, and it cannot be concatenated with a string, unless it is converted, due to that, we made use of the function str().

Conditionals

With the help of logical operators, and well, of logic in general, we will base ourselves in order to be able to use the instructions, because they will allow us to make more complex programs, since they allow us to set conditions, like what? Well, for example:

If it rains today, I take my sweater; if it doesn't rain, I don't take it.

In the same way, conditionals work, since an action is going to be carried out if a certain circumstance is fulfilled, but if the expected does not happen, something else will happen.

Among the conditionals, we will find the if, the else, and the elif; there are also the cases in which we use exceptions, which are used to prevent the program from collapsing.

- if statement: This is a simple conditional, if a certain circumstance happens, an action will be taken, otherwise nothing will happen and the usual or expected flow will continue. This can be used for simple programs such as access by age, How? Well, in case the client is not old enough, it will not let him get in.

The flowchart of the if conditional is as follows:

Now, the syntax of If in Python is as follows:

- If + condition: Then inside this block, with the required indentation, the following commands will be executed, obviously, if the condition is met.

Now some important things that have to be remembered when making the if blocks, in terms of syntax:
- The first line is always the if + condition, followed by a colon (:), since this way it is clear that a block is being started.

- The following lines indicate the instructions that will be fulfilled, but of course, obviously, they will occur in case the condition is true.

- Finally, it is the indentation that the block of instructions must have since in case these same are not placed correctly, the program will not understand what you specifically want and it will happen that it is not going to do what you requested or simply close the program.

A clearer example of the syntax is this, which will show whether a student passed an exam or not:

```
if.py                    ✕

1    note=input("Put your note here: ")
2    if(int(note)<5):
3        print("You didn't pass, try again")
4
```

As we can see here, a note variable was created, which is related to the input function, awaiting the note that the user obtained, this variable is of the string type.

Subsequently, we enter the conditional part, specifically the if, and the condition to compare is that, if the note that the user obtained is lower than five, then a screen will print that the user did not pass, and needs to try again.

As you can see, at the part of the if condition, the int() function was used, which is needed because the note variable is a string, and a comparison of a number with a string cannot be made, therefore it is necessary to change the type of string variable to integer, in order to make the corresponding comparison.

But what if the condition is false? Can you do another action? Well, you do, since there is another statement, and it is the else, which is used when the condition of the if is false and you need to do another action, then go to the usual flow, if you want to see this statement better explained, read the following paragraphs, which are responsible for explaining the statement.

- else + condition: The else condition is used when the if condition is false, what does this mean? This is nothing more than if the clause of the condition is not fulfilled, the program will close automatically; so that this does not happen we make use of the else instruction which will tell the program to perform another action.

The flowchart of the else conditional is the following:

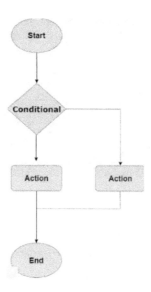

We can observe that the syntax of the conditional else is very similar to the syntax of the conditional if, only that, in this case, the conditional does not have to be placed, but it is of fundamental importance to maintain a correct indentation.

To observe in detail the programming of the else conditional, we will make a test program, in this way we will be able to see clearly the difference between conditionals.

It will be a modification to the past program, with the objective of showing how powerful the use of conditionals can be.

```
if.py

1   note=input("Put your note here: ")
2   if(int(note)<5):
3       print("You didn't pass")
4   else:
5       print("Congatulations, you pass")
6
```

In this example, we can see that the note variable was created, which is an entry that the user will choose, well, in this case, he will put his note, so that then the program will say if his note was enough to pass or not, so, to make clear to the user that he has to enter his note, the following string "Put your note here" will be printed on the screen, so the user knows that he has to put his note in the program.

After this, the conditional block was placed, in which the condition means that if the transformation to integer of the note entered by the user is less than five, "You didn't pass" will be printed on the screen, and then the program will end, since the block of the else will not be entered, because the condition is true. But if the condition is not true, it will be passed to else, which will print on the screen the next string "Congratulations, you passed", in order to show users that with their note they passed or not the exam.

As you could have observed, the use of if and else, is very useful, we would say that fundamental, because, thanks to it, you can make the program able to have different results and not have a single simple flow, because as you can guess, that type of programs that do not have logical bifurcations, are not widely used.

Another example that we can see is the division, with the same, we can see another very important utility of conditionals because the denominator cannot be equal to zero, because the division between zero is not defined and would be a mathematical error.

```python
num=input("Select the number of the numerator: ")
den=input("Select the number of the denominator: ")
if(den=="0"):
    print("Zero can't be denominator")
else:
    num=int(num)
    den=int(den)
    result=num/den
    print("The result is "+str(result))
```

Here we can see the example of the division since we have the problem previously explained.

The first thing is to create the variable num, it will be related to the numerator of the division, it will be declared next to an input function, so that the user enters the value he wants. Then the same will be done with the den variable, which is related to the denominator of the division.

Then we will enter the block of conditionals, the condition we will look for is that the variable den is equal to string "0", to know if, at the time of making the division, it can be or not. If the condition is true, the following string "Zero can't be denominator" will be printed on the screen, in order to show the user that the number he put as denominator does not meet the mathematical requirements. But, in the case that the condition is different from zero, the division can be done, therefore, we enter inside the else block; the first thing we do is to convert into integers the variable num and the variable den, but what is the objective of doing this in this part of the code? Well, to be able to do mathematical operations, both with num and den will have to be integers, but it is done in the part of the else, as a part of code optimization, because in the case that the denominator had been zero, time would have been spent on unnecessary instructions, because no operation was going to be performed, since the division between zero is not allowed, as you already know. At this moment, you will say that there is no difference between doing it here or not, but there is, imagine that you have to do that a million times, that would generate a big computational expense in something that is not going to be used, that is why it is always important to make this type of reasoning, in such a way that it is trying to make the program as optimal as possible.

The next action is to make the division between the numerator and the denominator, and this value will be stored in the result variable, to finally print the obtained result on screen.

If you are a little bit of a programmer, or already know how to program in C or Arduino, to say some languages, you will be waiting, in these explanations of the conditional sentences, the explanation of how the switch is used here, because in Python these are not found, in Python it is used the elif is used and its explanation can be seen below.

- elif + condition: We use the elif conditional as a faster and more effective way to join an else with elif for when there is more than one condition. For example: in other programming languages, it is very common to use the switch() conditional for multiple conditions. In the case of Python, this is replaced by elif(), this is nothing more than placing an additional conditional on the else to obtain multiple cases.

This is commonly used when you have multiple conditions, which have many different ways to perform.

Now, we will see an example to be able to understand in a very clear way how this works, and in this way, we will enter the conditionals.

```python
option=input("Please enter your option,for your message: \n1)Español \n2)English \n3)Deutsh \n")
if(option=="1"):
    print("Hola")
elif(option=="2"):
    print("Hello")
elif(option=="3"):
    print("Halo")
else:
    print("Bad option")
```

In the elif example, we can see that the option variable has been created, which is related to the option that the user wants to enter into his program, as can be seen in the code, the options are 1 for the answer to be in Spanish, 2 for the answer to be in English, and finally 3 for the answer of the program to be in German.

When entering the conditional block, the first thing we see is the if, which will have the condition that the variable option is the same strict as the string "1", if it is true, the string "Hello" will be shown on the screen; then, if this option is not fulfilled, it will go to the first elif, which will have a different condition, in this case is the one that says that the variable option is the same strict as the string "2", if this option is true, then it will show the message on screen, which says "Hello"; the last elif has the condition which indicates that the variable option has to be the same strict as the string "3", if it is true, it will proceed to send a message in German that says the following: "Halo". But if no case is fulfilled it will go to the else block, and this indicates that it will print in the console, a message that says "Bad option".

Therefore, we could see that the program has three options, and each one is a message that will be shown to the user saying hello in different languages, such as Spanish, German and English.

As we could see the examples of conditionals, we could see the great usefulness that they have in the programming, since they allow us to place an accumulation of options to our programs, and that they respond in a different way, depending on the situation.

But these conditionals are not the only ones that we can use for special conditions, another very useful tool, which is used a lot in programming, are the exceptions, as these catch any error, for the program to run in a correct way, moreover, in the example of division by zero you can use this tool, but not only for division by zero, but many more times, the only thing you need is the tools that you will see below.

Exception handling:

When we program, it is very frequent that we find errors during the execution of our programs. Two very common types of errors we might encounter on our way are syntax errors and exceptions. As we have already seen, syntax errors are those that occur when we enter code incorrectly.

In the case of exceptions, the syntax errors presented are different. How is this? Well, they happen while during the execution of a program something unexpected happens. For example, let's suppose a program in which we ask a user to enter a number to fill in a requirement. Now imagine that when the user is going to enter the data, he writes a string instead of a number, the program will automatically show a TypeError error.

When we don't handle exceptions properly, our program will close immediately because the interpreter won't know what to do in a special case like that.

Returning to the example shown above, we know that as long as we enter an integer value as an input value, our program will work correctly. However, if we enter a string the other type of error will be an exception to the ValueError type.

Some of the most common exceptions are:

NameError: The type of exception NameError, is the one that occurs when a program is not able to locate a global or local name. When the program is going to show us that it has not been possible to locate, it will include the wrong name in the message.

TypeError: The type of exception TypeError, is the one that occurs when an inappropriate object passes through the function as its argument. When the program is going to show us the type of error that has been presented, it will include in detail the correct ways to work with the arguments.

ValueError: The type of exception ValueError, is the one that occurs when an argument of the function contains its correct defined types, but its value is not adequate.

NotImplementedError: The type of exception NotImplementedError, is the one that occurs when an object that supports an operation has not been implemented. These types of errors are considered not to be used when a function supports an input argument, the most appropriate would be to use an exception of the TypeError type.

ZeroDivisionError: The ZeroDivisionError type of exception is one that occurs when a zero type of data is provided to the argument (such as a denominator) in a division operation or module operation.

FileNotFoundError: The FileNotFoundError exception type, is the one that occurs when a dictionary or file that has been requested is not existing in the program.

Handling exceptions: It is known that in each programming language there are certain quantities of reversed words, which make it easier for us to handle any exception that may arise when programming. In this way, we can take quick action to prevent the program from being interrupted.

In Python, when we handle exceptions we perform operations called "blocks", these blocks will be mostly used with the try, except & finally sentences.

So how does this work?

Raising the exception is going to happen in the following way: in the try block, you will find all the code, which could be raised with an exception. (It is known the term raise for programmers as the action of generating an exception.)

Once this is done, the exception block will be located, this is the one that will be in charge of enclosing the exception to obtain an opportunity to process it by sending a specific sample message.

Lastly, we have the finally block, which we are going to use to perform an action. This will be done no matter if the exception has been made or not, this way the block will be executed regardless of the previous conditions.

When we program exceptions the sentence finally is always considered very useful but many times there is not much emphasis on its importance.

Which is the finally block? What is it used for? What is it based on?

Let's suppose that we have written a code in the try block, it will take care of a certain task and will use a large amount of resources which have to be released once they cease to be used. These resources will be eliminated or released through the finally clause and the code will be executed without taking into consideration if the try block has been able to raise the exception it had.

As we know, it is not possible to make a division by zero, so we will use a similar example to show you how useful it is to work with exceptions.

```python
num=input("Please enter the numerator: ")
den=input("Please enter the denominator: ")
den= int(den)
nun=int(num)
try:
    result=num/den
    print("The result is: "+ srt(result))
except:
    print("Invalid values")
```

The first thing is to declare the variable num, which is related to the input function, it will be waiting for the data to be entered by the user, in such a way that a decimal value will be expected to be stored in num; in an analogous way, the same is done with the variable den, which is designed to be the denominator of the division.

The following action to all this, is to change the type of format of each variable, for it is used the function int(), to convert the variable num and den to integers, since as they are related to an input, the same ones will be stored as a string and it will be impossible to make arithmetic operations with them, for this reason, they are transformed to variables of type int.

Now we will enter the exceptions, since we first enter the try block, which is in charge, as its name indicates, of trying to do certain actions, if no exception occurs; what we mean by this is that, in this case, if den is not equal to zero, no exception should occur, therefore, the value of the division between num and den should be stored in the variable result, then the value of it will be printed on screen.

But in the case that some error occurs, specifically some exception, it will enter in the exceptions and will proceed to print in screen that the entered values are not valid.

Another example that we must show, is one which takes the block finally, so we can see its functionality, for this, we will continue with the examples of divisions, but now we are going to put two exceptions, one that will appear in the case that the values that are entered are not decimal, therefore, it will be impossible to convert these data into integers, for this reason, the first exception will be triggered. Then it will be verified if the denominator is equal to zero, and if it is true, another exception will have to be thrown.

```
execp.py ×

1   num=input("Please enter the numerator: ")
2   den=input("Please enter the denominator: ")
3   try:
4       den= int(den)
5       num=int(num)
6   except:
7       print("Error, you put a ASCII data, please try again")
8       num=int(input("Please enter the numerator: "))
9       den=int(input("Please enter the denominator: "))
10  try:
11      result=num/den
12      print("The result is: "+str(result))
13  except:
14      print("Error, the den has a value equal to zero")
15  finally:
16      print("Thanks for use this program")
17
```

Here we can see better the example, the first thing we see, and that we should expect, is that both the variable num, and the variable den, are using the input() function, which will be in charge of receiving the value that the user wants, in this case, the value of the numerator and the denominator respectively.

Then we enter the first block of instructions, What are we trying to do in this section? The first thing is to convert the strings that are both num and den, to integer variables in order to continue with the relevant mathematical operations, for this reason, it is important to make the type transformation, because as you know, it is not possible to divide a letter between another letter, because mathematically it does not make sense. The first thing is the try block, which as its name indicates, will try to do something, if there is not anything that generates some error, then it will do it without any problem, but in the case that it is not possible to do that, then it will enter inside the block except, which will be in charge of processing the exception. That block, in case, that an error has been found, will enter in action since it will try to fix the error found, the first thing it will do is to show in screen the error, it will transmit to you that erroneous ASCII data was placed, that please try again. Then the num variable will be Redeclared, which will be input type since it will be waiting for the values entered by the user, and then it will be transformed to an integer type variable, the same will be done with the den variable.

Later, the other block of exceptions will be entered, the first instruction we find in it is to declare the result variable, which will be the division between the num and den; to then place on the screen the result of the division. And well, as you should know, this block will try to do that, but there is the possibility of an error, but what could it be? Well, the main one is the division by zero, more than a programming error, it is a mathematical error, therefore, this block cannot be executed and the part of the exception will be entered. The same one will try to communicate to the user that an error exists, this message will say to him that the denominator has a value equal to zero, for this reason, it is not going to be possible to execute the division.

At last, we will enter the finally block, which will make an instruction no matter what happens, no matter if the try or the excepts are executed, this block will always be executed. It, in this case, will print a message, in which it will be thankful to have used this program.

But if you verify the previous example and this one, the block finally does not do anything very special, but it does, the difference is that this is always done, now, if you want to get an example, in which is used more and is more important the finally, you will see it when you use the databases, because always, whatever happens, it is essential to close the connection to a database, because if this is not done, it may cause some errors that any programmers want to have.

Chapter 4: Loops

What is a Loop?

A loop (or cycle), is a control structure that is in charge of repeating a block of instructions, while a certain condition is fulfilled, within the loops we also have the so-called infinite loops in which their condition is never fulfilled. As in most programming languages, Python has a while and for.

1. Loop For: Python's for statement iterates on the items of any sequence (either a list, a string of characters or dictionary), in the order they appear in the sequence. Where the code is called "loop body" and its repetitions "iterations".

Where iteration is defined by performing a number of actions repeated times. The for loop is in charge of going through these actions in order to look for elements that fulfill certain conditions and that at the same time can carry out the specified instructions. So all these elements must be iterable.

The syntax of a for loop is as follows:
for variable + an iterable element (list, string, range, etc.) :
loop body.

It is necessary to specify the variable in which the items of the element are going to be saved, then we write our sentence for with a variable that will store the items and finally we write in which will be our element to iterate.

The loop is executed as long as it fulfills a condition, so once the iteration is finished, this will make the loop stop.

Example:

```
1    x=0
2    for x in range(4):
3        print(x)
4    print("End")
5
```

The first thing we can see is that we define the variable x, which starts at zero, this is because it is going to iterate, and must start with zero.

Then we fully enter the for cycle, and as you can see, it is specified that the variable x, is going to iterate within the range of 4, What does this mean? Well, x is going to iterate four times and take the value of zero, one, two and three.

The next part is the block inside the for, which is a simple print, and this is going to show us the value that has x in each part of the for, until it gets to be valued four, when it has that value, it will automatically quit the cycle.

Finally, End will be written to show that the program is finished and the cycle was quit.

Types of for loops:

1. Loop "for" with lists: you can make for cycles with lists, in this case, it will iterate within each value of the list.
In order to better understand what we are talking about, we will make some examples of each one of these ways of using the for.

a. Loop "for" with list and the function "range"; in this loop are presented list data types and with the help of the function len() and range(), it is possible to make a for, these are very useful to print data.

-range() is a function that, as mentioned above, returns a list of integers, accepting as arguments the beginning of the list, the end and the increment between one element and the next. We can also omit one or two of them, as explained below;
- range (n); this type of function takes care of returning a list of integers beginning with 0 and ending in n-1.
- range (beginning, end); this type of function is in charge of returning the list of integers located between the beginning and the end, without including the latter.

- range (beginning, end, step); this type of function takes charge of returning the list of integers, as in the previous case, only that between the beginning and the next element will exist a difference of step, and so on.

Let's do two examples, one without the range function, and another with it.

1) Use of for and lists, without the use of range:

```
 for.py        ✕

1    sports=['soccer', 'baseball','tennis','polo']
2    for x in sports:
3        print(x)
4    print("End")
5
```

As you can see in the example, first, a list was created, which has the name sports, it has as items, different sports, such as soccer, baseball, tennis, and polo.

Subsequently, the for cycle was defined, and, What does the x variable do this time? What it does is iterate within the sports list, so x will take the values of each item it has within the list.

The next thing is to define the for block, it is important to remember the indentation because if this is not done, no action will be done because Python takes this very seriously. Since we already placed the indentation, we define the block, which is a simple print, and what this does is print the values of x, and well, as we have already explained, x will take the value of the items from the list in question.

And well, to finish, will be printed on-screen "End", to show that the program has finished and quit the cycle correctly.

2) Use of for and lists, with the use of range:

```
  for.py        ●

1    sports=['soccer', 'baseball','tennis','polo']
2    for x in range(len(sports)):
3        print("The sport "+str(x+1)+" is "+sports[x])
4    print("End")
5
```

In the example, we can see a change; the first one is that in this case we use the range, but we are going to go step by step to explain the code and make it very simple.

The first thing, as we have already seen, is to make a list, in this case, the same list of the previous example, with the consequences that this entails, this means that the items of the previous example, will be the same as the current ones.

Then, we define the for, in this case, we place the range, with which we mean that x iterate from zero to the range of numbers that the len function returns to us, but, what does this mean? Well, x is going to iterate within a list of the length that the len function tells us, therefore, if len returns a value of four, then the variable x will iterate from zero to three, taking the values zero, one, two, three, and as you can see, it will iterate four times, as the len function said, of course, if it gives us a value of four.

Afterward, we programmed the for block, which is a print, but in this case, "The sport" was printed, then it was concatenated with the string that returned the function str(x+1), but, why x+1? Because as x varies from zero to the number that gives us the function range, the first position of the sport will be zero, for that reason, we added one, and so it will appear on the screen, that the first sport, is in position one. After this, it is concatenated with " is " and it is also concatenated with sport[x], in this case, as if it is a list, it is concatenated with the item of the position x of the list, and these positions go from zero to the value n-1 of range.

And finally, "End" was printed on the screen, to say that the program has finished, and the for cycle was finished correctly.

It is important to remember, that for the variable x to vary, this has to iterate within a list, and as it has been said before, the function range returns a list of m numbers, therefore if we say that a = range(10), we can obtain that a will be equal to [0, 1, 2, 3, 4, 5, 6, 7, 8, 9], therefore, the variable x will vary from zero to nine.

b. Loop "for" with Tuples; tuples are sequence objects, specifically, it is an immutable list data type, so it cannot be modified after its creation. This type of program is not very difficult to design, since, to program in tuples and cycles, it is done in a similar way that with lists, the only detail is to keep in mind the difference that exists between list and tuple.

Two examples will be shown in the same way, the first one will be with range and the other one will obviate this function.

1) Loop for with Tuples and range:

```
🐍 for.py        ✕

1    foods=("pizza", "hot dog", "sushi")
2    x=0
3    for food in range(len(foods)):
4        print("The x value is: "+str(x))
5        print("The food value is: "+str(food))
6        print("The foods item is: "+foods[food])
7        x+=1
8    print("End")
9
```

Here the first thing we see is that we create the tuple foods, which has some items within it, among which are the strings "pizza", "hot dog" and "sushi", and as you should know, after creating a tuple, it cannot be modified, or changed, or anything like that.

Then a variable x was declared, which has the assigned value of zero.

Next step is to declare the for, and as you can see, in this case, it is not going to iterate the variable x, but a food variable, which is going to iterate within the list that is going to return the range function, which should give a list of three elements, and, Why three elements? Well, as you already know, the len function returns the value of the length of a list or a tuple, and as in this case, the tuple foods has three elements, then the range function should create a tuple that goes from zero to two.

Then, to see more clearly how the variable food iterates, the following instructions were programmed, first the value that has the variable x was printed in that instant, then, the value of food was printed in that instant, with the objective of verifying if they have the same value, and as you already know, to concatenate an integer with a string, the function str was used. Next act is to print the item of the corresponding food, for that reason "The food item is: " is concatenated with foods[food], since we can select a specific value of the tuple foods, and well, in this case, it will be the one that is in the food position. Last but not least, it is said that x will be updated to the next value.

To finalize the code, the string "End" will be printed in the console, to make it clear that the program has finished and that it ended in a correct way.

2) Loop for with Tuples and without range:

```
for.py    ×

1    messages=("Hello", "my", "name", "is", "Marco")
2    for message in messages:
3        print(message)
4    print("End")
5
```

In this example, we can see that it is very nice since we send a message with the tuple, but how does this work? Well...

First, we create the tuple messages, which has the following items, "Hello", "my", "name", "is", "Marco", as we can see, is a tuple of five items, therefore it has a length of five.

Next step is to create the for, in this case, the variable message, it will iterate inside the tuple messages; Then the variable message will be printed, in the position that it is, with which, you will be able to infer that each message will be printed with a line break.

And finally, as it has been done in the previous examples, it will be printed in console "End' to show that it has left the cycle and the program is finished.

c. Loop "for" with dictionary; the dictionary defines a one-to-one relationship between keys and values, the dictionary type objects allow a series of operators integrated in the Python interpreter for its management.

Analogous to the loops explained above, this "for" loop with dictionary is worked in a very similar way, since all these types of data are similar. But it is worth mentioning that they are different types and are treated in a different way, therefore, even if they are handled similarly, it should never be forgotten that they are different types of data.

Example:

```
for.py

1   clothes={"shirt":"red", "shoes":"black","pant":"blue"}
2   for key in clothes:
3       print(key)
4   clothe=input("Choose one of them: ")
5   if(clothe in clothes):
6       print("Your clothe is "+clothe+ " of color "+clothes[clothe])
7   else:
8       print("Error")
9
```

In this example we can see how to work with dictionaries; with the variable we created called clothes, which, as you know, is a dictionary. This has the items "shirt", which has a value associated with "red", there is also "shoes", which is related to "black", and finally "pant", which relates to "blue".

After that, we created the for cycle, which tells us that the key variable will iterate in all the values of the clothes dictionary. And if you run this code, in your favorite text editor, you will note that the key variable, will only have associated the values of "shirt", "shoes" and "pant", this can be observed, because the cycle inside the for, what it does is to print the key-value inside the dictionary.

Then, we create the clothe variable, which is a variable that will receive an input, which will depend on the user. When receiving the user's value, an if will be made, and in the case that the variable clothe is inside clothes, as you can see in the condition of the if, it will be entered there, and it will be printed that "Your clothe is" + the option chosen by the user + "of color "+ clothes[clothe]; but what are clothes[clothe]? It is the value associated with the clothe selected by the user, better said, if the user chooses "pant", then clothes[clothe] will throw the value of "blue".

Finally, the else condition means that if no clothe is found inside clothes, then "Error" will be printed, and this is very useful since if no value is found inside a database, it will be thrown that the requested value is found or not.

2. Loop "While"; it allows us to execute cycles or periodic sequences that allow us to do things multiple times in a row. This cycle will allow us to execute a block continuously, as long as the while condition is true, and by this, we mean "True". This loop will be in charge of evaluating the condition and if it is correct, the loop is executed and the condition is checked again at the end and if it is still true "True", the program will be executed again, if this condition is not correct "False", it will be omitted and the common execution of the program will be carried out.

There are several types of "while" loops; like the "while" loop controlled by counting, the infinite while and others; all very useful in specific conditions.

Its syntax is very simple, and is as follows:
While (condition):
Block of instructions within the cycle

Now let's make a simple example, which will consist of the cycle printing a number, as many times as the user wants.

Example:

```
1   cycles=input("Put the number of cycles here: ")
2   count=0
3   while(count<int(cycles)):
4       count+=1
5       print("Cycle number "+str(count))
6   print("End")
7
```

In this example, we can observe several things, the first is that we create a variable cycles, which is an entry, which will allow us, as users to enter the number of cycles we want to do in this program, of course, you must never forget that this type of entry is a string, therefore, to do mathematical operations, it is necessary to transform this type of input.

Then another variable will be created, called count, which has a fundamental function, and it is to be the cycle counter of our program, with which we define that the same one will begin in zero, for then, to start the count.

The next action is, to begin with the while cycle, as we can see in the syntax previously explained, first it is declared that we are going to make a while, then, between the parentheses we have the condition.

a. Loop "while" controlled by counting; in this cycle, there is a counter, and this counter will increase as the cycles are carried out, this process will be repeated as many times as necessary until the expected number is reached. We will understand this loop better with the example that we will see next.

Although we have already seen an example of the while controlled by counting, that was the last one, it is never too much to take another example, the same through the counting method, in this case, we are going to make the counter go from higher to lower, as we will see below.

```
while.py    ×

1    cycles=input("Put the number of cycles here: ")
2    a=int(cycles)
3    while(0<a):
4        a-=1
5        print("Cycles to end "+str(a))
6    print("End")
7
```

In this example, we make a turn of one hundred and eighty degrees, because the counter does not have to reach the maximum value, but starts in it and is going to decrease.

The first thing is that a variable called cycles is created, which is related to an input that the user will write, in which he will enter the number of cycles he wants to do. Next act is to create a variable a, which needs the function int(), since it turns the variable cycles into an integer, because as you should know, the variable cycles is a string, since the entries are saved that way, and with the strings it is not possible to perform arithmetic operations.

In the following line, we declare the while loop, and as it can be observed, the condition is that zero has to be lower strictly than a, therefore, in the moment that a is equal to zero, the cycle will be exited and the other instruction will be passed.

Then, inside the block of instructions that are inside the cycle, the variable a has to be decreased, this is done through the instruction a-=1, which is equivalent to saying that a = a - 1, and it can be observed easily as the variable a is decreased by a unit.

The next instruction is to print on screen the following message "Cycles to end" concatenated with the number of missing cycles to exit the cycle.

Finally, the "End" string is placed on the screen to say that the program has finished and that the while was exited correctly.

This type of cycles by counts are very useful, we are going to use them first with the utility of those cycles in which it is necessary that the counter grows, the first utility that comes to our head is to make a programmed chronometer, in such a way that when arriving at the maximum value, it is going to leave the cycle and show in screen that the required time has been fulfilled, now, there are also other utilities as it can be to check a list with a known length, therefore we will be moving item by item; although this last utility easily can be replaced by a loop for. Now, while cycles per count, but in this case, that the counter goes decreasing, could be used to make a countdown to sound an alarm or something like that.

b. Infinite "while" loop: This type of while is very useful, in the case that an accumulation of instructions is done a number of times not determined, with this we mean that we do not know how many times it is going to be done, therefore the programmer, will make the condition a while(True), and of course, as you can see, the True boolean, allows the while to work constantly.

Let's code two examples, one that we use an infinite while, the strict way, and another not so much, although the programmer does not know the number of cycles that will be done, does not use the True condition to force the block to be repeated indefinitely.

Examples:

1) While with the True condition:

```
while.py    ✕

1    import time
2    x=1
3    while(True):
4        print(x)
5        x+=1
6        time.sleep(1)
7
```

The first thing we observe that is different is the import of the time module, but those are issues that we will see later, at this time is not something very important.

Now what really interests us is the declaration of the variable x as one since this will work as a kind of counter, so it will increase little by little.

The next step is to create or, better said, declare the while, and as you can see, the condition inside the while is True, therefore, it will always be fulfilled, which indicates that the cycle will be repeated at all times, unless some sentences are declared, which we will see later.

Inside the while block, the variable x will be printed on the screen, and this is where it makes sense to use x as a counter since it will allow us to see in the console the specific second that has happened since the program started. Then it increases the value of x, because as we have already said, it has a counter function, and it will increase one by one.

Finally, we use the library time, so that will make a delay of a second, that's why our program works as a chronometer, which will show us on screen the second in which we are after running the code, and the same will be updated every second.

Sentences used in the while loop:

1. Break Sentence: the word break is used to interrupt the cycles or abandon the cycles even when they have not finished, meaning that the evaluated expression of while remains in the true position. To be able to evaluate and understand this sentence, let's see the following example.

```python
while True:
    x=input("Put one to break of the while cycle: ")
    if(x=="1"):
        break
    print("You dont put the one, please try again")
print("End")
```

In this example, we see how to implement infinite while cycles, because as you can see in the first line, the condition inside the while is always going to be true, therefore we are in front of an infinite cycle.

Later, we declare the variable x, which is related to the input function, which will be waiting for the user to enter any value, specifically, it is necessary to enter a one so that it exits the cycle, in case that what user enters is not the indicated value, then the cycle will be repeated.

As you can see in line three, you have a statement of an if, which asks if x is equal to the string "1", Why is it compared with a string? Because, as we already know, x is a string because it is related to the input function, at the moment in which this variable is declared. If the condition is true, the "break" sentence will be used, which specifies us to exit the infinite cycle.

If the condition is not true, then the following string "You don't put the one, please try again" will be printed on the screen.

Finally, at the moment of exiting the cycle, the usual "End" will be printed, to show that the cycle was executed correctly, and the program was finished.

What we can learn from our example with the break? or what benefit we can get from it? Well, the first thing is that the sentence break is extremely useful to get out of the cycles, it does not have to be strictly an infinite cycle, because it can be used in a cycle that is operated by counting or another method, therefore, it is important to remember that. Another fundamental thing is that this type of sentence, not only works for a while but can also be used in for cycles, therefore, are an essential tool when programming.

But in what cases should this type of statement be used? Well, the first case that comes to mind is the handling of some exception that may occur within the cycles, in the event that something unwanted occurs, it gets out of it and notifies the error or does what you desire to program. Another case may be an access system since a specific key was requested, and in the case that the correct key is not entered, the user will not be allowed to enter another part of the program.

2. Sentence Continue: This sentence ends up being very useful when programming, when applying it we will be omitting what follows the sentence within the cycle. That is to say, if we fulfill some previous conditions, as, for example, if after several "if" or else, or other steps, we manage to reach a continue sentence, we will proceed to omit the rest of the instructions of the cycle,

and then do another iteration. We could summarize that the instruction continues inside a loop forces the interpreter to return to the beginning of the loop ignoring all the instructions and interactions that are inside it.

The next example will show a while cycle, which will omit the values that are multiples of five, if these values are multiples, then it will not be printed on screen and the next iteration will be done automatically.

```python
cycles=input("Please put the numer of cycles: ")
count=1
while(count-1<int(cycles)):
    a=count
    count+=1
    if(a%5 == 0):
        print("Error, continue")
        continue
    else:
        print("Not is multiple of 5")
    print(a)
print("End")
```

To start, the variable cycles is created, which is an input, which asks the user to enter the number of cycles he wants to do, and, as is well known, you have that cycles is a string.

Next, it creates the variable count, which is integer type, this will have the function of counter, to know the cycle in which we are, to reach the maximum level that the user wants.

Now we will create the while loop, which specifies that count-1 has to be lower than cycles, and, Why count -1? Well, in order to fulfill what the user wants; since if the condition was, a lower or equal to cycles, the code will be less optimal, for this reason, only a strict lower is placed, and as the counter starts in one, it is necessary to subtract a unit and that the number of corresponding cycles is met.

In the following line, the variable a is declared, which has the same count value, because to know the current value of the cycle, and well, as it is obvious, the counter is increased by one unit, through the instruction in line five, which says count += 1.

Subsequently, one enters the block of conditionals, in this case, the condition is a% 5 ==0, but what does this mean? Well, the rest that gives the division between a and five, has to be strictly equal to zero, in order to enter the if. In the case that the condition is true, the orders found in the if block will be performed, these instructions are the following; the first thing is to print on screen that there was an error, then the continue sentence will be used. If this condition is false, the instruction containing the else block will be passed, which is based on notifying that the cycle is a multiple of five.

At the end of the conditionals, the cycle number is printed on the screen to know when we are in the program.

And finally, a screen print is placed to show that the program has been completed and the cycle was exited correctly.

Now, what can we learn from this program? The first thing is the use of the continue, because its function, specifically is to go directly to the next while cycle, omitting the other lines of the block, well, in this case, it is the same, since when arriving at the continue we pass to the other cycle, but in the case that this sentence is not found, the value of a would be printed, as you can see that it is the next instruction after the conditional block, but this type of sentences, interrupt the natural flow of the program, being very useful for the handling of some exception that happens within the cycles.

3. Pass Sentence: It is a null expression, in other words, this sentence does nothing, but it allows us to create a loop without placing code in its body to be able to add it later and use it in this way as a temporary filler, with this we mean to add some type of delay to the program; or as well in the case that you manage

the programming with assembler or with processors, it is a way to make a nop. It is a sentence that will not affect in anything the behavior of the code, and it should be noted that not only can be used in cycles, it can also be used anywhere in the code without any problem, with these words, we mean that the sentence can also be used in a common function without any trouble, but this is not worth to mention yet, because we have not seen functions, but it is not excessive to know that the pass can be implemented with the functions. We could say to establish a difference that continues will take care of ending the current interaction, but will continue with the next iteration of that loop, going back to the beginning, while pass is not going to do anything, just continue with the following instructions without going back to the beginning. Next, let's see an example of what it is.

```python
while.py    ×

1    cycles=input("Please put the numer of cycles: ")
2    count=1
3    while(count-1<int(cycles)):
4        a=count
5        count+=1
6        if(a%5 == 0):
7            print("Error, continue")
8            pass
9        else:
10           print("Not is multiple of 5")
11       print(a)
12   print("End")
13
```

By looking at the previous example, we can see how we declare the variable cycles, which is going to wait for the user to specify how many cycles to use, the input will be of the string type.

Then the count counter will be created, which will start from one for convenience, but has the function of knowing what is the current position of the cycle.

The following order, is the creation of the while cycle, with the condition that count-1, has to be strictly lower than int(cycles), it is worth noting that the use of the int() function, since the cycles variable is of string type and making comparisons with strings and integers is not possible since they are different types of data. The reason of the count- 1 is explained in the previous example, so we don't have to repeat it, but remember that we are making comparisons starting from zero and that is the reason why the comparison is strictly lower and is not lower or equal since we would make one more cycle.

The following instructions are to declare the variable a, which will be assigned the value of count, this is to be able to make operations on this value and not lose it; then the value of count will be increased by one unit, since if this variable is not increased, we will be doing the same thing infinitely.

The next part is the conditional phase, which is in charge of verifying if it is a multiple of five, and we do this by using the "%" operator since it will return the rest of the division we place, so that if we place, for example 10% 3, it will return the value of 1, which is the rest; in an analogous way it is done here, since when putting the following instruction a% 5, we are asking for the rest between these values, and to know if a number is a multiple of another, because the rest between both should be zero, for this reason, the strict equality is made to zero, in the case that the condition is fulfilled, because we will be in front of a number that is divisible by five, or multiples of five, being those the numbers that we want to find.

Now in such a case that the if condition is met, we will proceed to make a cumulus of instructions, the same will be, to print in screen that an error has been produced and that it is going to continue, then, the following instruction is the sentence pass, which will not do anything, is like causing a small delay in the program, depending on the frequency of the clock of the processor of our machine, but those are subjects that do not interest us very much. But, if the condition is false, then it will enter inside the block of the else, and this only will print that this number of the cycle is not multiple of the five.

Now, at the moment that the conditional block was finished, therefore, it does not matter if the condition is true or false, the number of the cycle in which we are will be printed on screen, by the command print(a), because a is the current position.

Finally, when exiting the while cycle, the "End" string will be printed on the screen, which indicates that the while loop has been correctly exited and the program has been completed.

Now, when trying to find a utility to the pass sentence, you don't really find many at this moment that you haven't seen the functions, since now it's just a delay, but it's not a delay appreciable by the user, since the computer clock frequency is in GHz, therefore it's so fast that it's not appreciable, but when you see the functions, there will be times when a complex program is being developed, and there are parts that have not been created, but for the program to work it already had to have created the functions, but the body of the functions has not yet been developed, which is why the use of these sentences is important, so that our software does not break, for saying so.

Chapter 5: Functions

A function is basically a portion or block of reusable code that performs a given task. It is a code block with an associated name, which receives arguments as input, in addition, follows a sequence of sentences, which executes a desired operation and then returns a value and perform a task, this block can be called when we need, and this can be considered a great advantage. Python is a language that gives us a lot of flexibility when creating these functions.

The use of these functions is a very important component within the paradigm of programming called structured and therefore has several advantages:

* It allows reusing the same function in different programs, therefore, when it does the functions, it is not necessary to repeat the code a lot of times.
* It allows segmenting a complex program in modules that are simpler, and in this way, we will have an easier programming, as well as a more facilitated debugging, it is as the saying goes, "Divide and conquer", therefore, it is a very used technique.

The Python programming language has what we call functions integrated into the language, which allows us to create functions defined by the user himself to be used later in his own program. These functions are presented below:

Function	Use	Example	Result
Print ()	This function allows the program to print in screen the desired argument	Print ("Hello")	"Hello"
Len ()	This function allows you to determine the length of the characters that a string contains	Len ("Hello world")	11
Join()	This function allows you to convert a string to	List=['Python', 'is'] '-'. Join (List)	'Python-is'

	another by using "-"		
Split()	This function will let you convert a string into a list	A=("This will be a list") List2= a.split()	A=['This', 'will', 'be', 'a', 'list']
Replace()	This function, as it names indicates, will let you replace a string for another	Text= "The house is green" Print (Text) Text= Text.replace("green", "yellow") Print(Text)	"The house is green" "The house is yellow"
Upper() and lower()	This function allows us to convert into upper or lower case all the letters in a string	Text= "The house is green" Text.upper() Print (Text) Text.lower() Print(Text)	"THE HOUSE IS GREEN" "the house is green"

Ord()	This function will let you use ASCII data type	Print (ord('A'))	65
Tuple()	This function will convert a string into a tuple	Words= tuple ("I am old") Print(Words)	('I', 'a', 'm', 'o', 'l', 'd')
Type()	This function will return the type of data of an element	X=5 Print(type(X))	<class 'int'>
List ()	This function will let you create lists from an element	Word= list('Hello') Print (Word)	['H', 'e', 'l', 'l', 'o']
Round ()	This function will round the decimal	Print (round(15,746))	16

	part of a number to its nearest integer		
Str()	This function will convert a numerical value into a string	X=5 A=str(X) Print (A)	"5"
Range()	This function will create a list of n elements. It is mainly used in the for cycle	X=range(3) Print(X)	[0, 1, 2]
Float ()	This function will allow us to convert any value to a decimal type of value	A=float("5.55") Print(A)	5.55

Max() & Min()	These functions will determinate the higher and the lower values in a set of numbers	X= [2, 6, 3, 8, 0] Print (max(X)) Print(min(X))	8 0
Sum()	This function will add the numbers of a set of numbers	X=[3, 1, 6] Print(sum(X))	10
Int()	This function will convert any value into an integer	A=("35") Print (int(A))	35

What rules do I have to follow to be able to define a function?

- The input parameters must be defined within the parenthesis of the function.

- When we develop the code, we must identify the indentation very well and correctly (4 characters of space).

- The code of the function will always start after we place the colon. ": "

It should be noted that a function will not be executed until it is invoked, and to be able to invoke a function it must be called by its name. For example:

```
function.py

1    a=[1, 2, 3, 4, 5]
2    b=[1, 0, 1, 0, 1]
3    num="5 6 7 8 9"
4    c=num.split()
5    print(c)
6    e=[]
7    for x in c:
8        d=int(x)
9        e.append(d)
10   c=e
11   d=[]
12   for x in range(len(a)):
13       e=a[x]+b[x]+c[x]
14       d.append(e)
15   e=min(d)
16   f=max(d)
17   g=sum(d)
18   print(a)
19   print(b)
20   print(c)
21   print(d)
22   print(e)
23   print(f)
24   print(g)
25
```

As we can see in this example, which is quite complete, at first we created variables a and b, they are lists, which have within them integer values, specifically five items, a is a list of numbers ranging from one to five, while b is an iteration of values of ones and zeros.

The second, is the creation of the variable num, it is a string, in which is written "5 6 7 8 9", and as we saw previously, the function split(), creates an arrangement of strings, each item will be a word, separated by white space, in the code, specifically in line four, we make use of this function, in which we convert the variable c, in a list of strings, which should have the form ["5", "6", "7", "8", "9"], but it is not possible to do mathematical operations with this type of data, as they are, to be more specific, as strings, therefore we are going to proceed to convert all these items into integers, so that you verify that it is true what we say here, we use the print of the list c, so that you can see the list of strings.

To achieve our goal, first we declare the variable e as an empty list, then we use a for cycle, in which the variable x, will iterate within the array c, which has its items as strings, therefore, within a variable d, the integer that results after applying the function int() to the element of the list c at that time. Then the value of d is added, within the list e, until the number of iterations is finished. The next action is to store in c, the list that was stored in e, in order to have a better order of the variables.

Subsequently, the variable d was assigned the value of an empty list, in order to store data within it. Then, with the help of a for, which is going to iterate as many times as the number of items in the list a, as we are going to have to move through all its items, since what we want is to create another list, which contains the sum of a, b and c, so inside the same buble, it is said that e will be equal to the sum of the item that is in position x, of lists a, b and c. After adding the three items, the append function will be used to add the value obtained to the d list.

How to create your own function?

To be able to create a function of our own, we must follow the "def" sentence and proceed to name it, except that this time it will not be the name of a predefined function, but this time it will have a name created by us.

How can I call a function?

To be able to call a function, we only have to declare it when we start in our code. This is fundamental because it is not possible to invoke a function that has not been created in advance. Example:

Parameters

We define parameters as a type of value that is entered into the function when the function is invoked, a function may be able to receive one or more parameters. These parameters must be separated by a comma "," in order to be invoked.

Example:

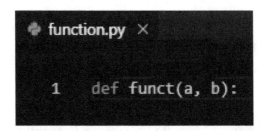

As you can see in this small example, because it is very simple, really, it was just to show how the first part of a function should be defined.

The sentence that can never be missing when defining a function is the def, which is the one that specifies that a function is going to be created or, better said, indicates that a function is being defined.

Then we can see that follows a word, in this case, funct, that word was to put a name to our function, and then you can see a parenthesis, which has two letters, a and b, meaning that these are going to be the parameters that our function will receive to work.

How can we define arguments and parameters?

As we already know, we call parameters to the values that the function receives when it is defined. When the function is invoked, these values are called arguments and divided according to their type.

These arguments are divided into several types:

Arguments by name:

When we are going to invoke a function, we must indicate in the arguments the value that each parameter will contain starting from its name.

```python
def funct(a, b):
    return a+b

c=funct(b=5, a=3)
print(c)
```

As we can see, we continue with the funct function, in this case, we still have the same parameters a and b, we also see how the definition is exactly the same, the only difference is at line two, as it indicates that the sum of a with b is going to return. The return sentence will be explained later, but it is not something too complicated, the same name tells us what it does, to return a value.

Then in the following lines, the variable c is created, which will be equal to the value returned by the function we have created, and as we said previously, it will be equal to the sum of its parameters a and b. As you can see, when you call the function in line four, first write the name of the function, in this case funct, and the arguments that are going to be passed, are previously specified with the name, as you can see, the argument that has a value of five, is specified that it will be parameter b of the funct function, analogously is done with parameter a.

Finally, the value of c is printed on the screen, so that you can visualize that the result is correct.

Argument by position:

When we send an argument to a function, they receive the defined parameters in order.

```
● function.py ×

1    def hello(name, color):
2        print("Hello "+name+ " your favorite color is "+color)
3
4    a=input("What is your name? ")
5    b=input("What is your favorite color? ")
6    hello(a,b)
7
```

In this example, another function will be created, which is called hello, and has as parameters both name and color, this function was created to make a message on screen, in which the user will be greeted with his name and will also be told what is his favorite color.

To call this function first it is necessary to declare two variables, the first one is the variable a, who is in charge of storing the value of the string related to the user's name, while b, is in charge of storing the string related to the user's favorite color, these variables are related to the input function, which means that they will be waiting for the user to enter the value he wants.

Finally, the hello function is called, making use of its name, but in this case, the arguments were passed by order and not by name, so you have to be very aware for the correct order, since, if there is an error in this, the program can easily collapse or fail to do what is required.

As you could see, the ways to pass the arguments are different, you can use the one you prefer, it depends on your preferences; in the case that you find it easier or faster by position do it that way, but take into account that you have to be aware that the argument is in the correct parameter position, but if you like it more by name, do it that way, of course, you also have to be aware that you are writing the parameter names correctly.

Call without arguments

When we call a function that has some defined parameters, if these are not passed correctly an error will be generated.

```
function.py ×

1    def hello():
2        print("Hello")
3
4    hello()
5
```

In this example, the hello function is created, which is not going to have parameters, and this will only make a screen print, with the message "Hello".
Then, to call it, only the name of the function will be written with parentheses, in the following way name().

Return statement

As we have seen before, most Python functions will contain a return value which can be explicit or implicit.

We know that return is a reserved word whose purposes are to finish the execution of some function and then return the value obtained as a result.

If you want to visualize an example of this, you can see the one that is in arguments by position, since it can be observed that the function has the return sentence, which will return the value of the sum of a plus b; and also, as you can observe in this example, that value is stored in the variable c, to then print it.

Lambda function

We define lambda functions as a special type of function which is part of the predefined functions in Python. What do we mean by this? This type of function is mainly noted for being "exclusive" because it allows us to create "anonymous" functions quickly because it has a somewhat exclusive syntax.

The lambda functions are able to execute an expression and return the result of it, it can contain optional parameters in its structure, but nevertheless, this function has its own restrictions.

Syntax of the lambda function

The syntax of the lambda function in Python is very simple since it is based only on writing the reserved word lambda, followed by the arguments that come with the action and finally separating with their respective double point ":".

```python
1    sum= lambda x,y: x+y
2    a=sum(3,10)
3    print(a)
```

In this example, we see the use of the function lambda, in this case to the variable sum, we make use of the sentence lambda, in order to create a function that has as purpose to make the sum of two numbers, both x and y. For that reason, it is observed that the parameters that we have is the one of x and y; for then inside the block of the function, return the sum of both.

Finally, to call the function, to the variable that we declared as a, we assigned the value that returns sum, for then, to make sure that the result is certain, we proceeded to print in screen the value that stores the variable a, and if you get to run this program, you will be able to observe that it will give 13.

The lambda function is commonly used when you need to invoke a function for a short time (this function does not require a name) and is mostly used together with the integrated functions filter(), map().

Filter() function

The filter() function is the one (as its name indicates) that is in charge of filtering. What does this mean? This function takes a sequence as arguments, either a list or an iterator, then it will return an iterable with the elements already filtered (this will return a true if the condition is met).

```python
def pair(n):
    if(n>0 and n%2==0):
        return True
    else:
        return False

numbers=[]
for x in range(25):
    numbers.append(x)

pairs=filter(pair, numbers)

for x in pairs:
    print("The number "+str(x)+" is pair")
```

For this example, the first thing we need is a conditional function, to know what we are going to filter, in our case, we will create the pair function, which will have as parameter, the integer n, then we enter a conditional block, in the part of the if, the condition would be that n has to be higher than zero, since the zero is a number that is not even, the other condition that must be fulfilled at the same time, is that the rest of the division between n and two has to be strictly equal to zero, because as you should know, this is the definition of a pair number.

The next step is to fill our arrangement of numbers that we are going to filter, for it we create the variable numbers, which will be an empty list. To then enter a for loop, in which a variable x will vary from zero to 24, as you can see in line 8, this is thanks to the range function, which gives us the limits of the for. The next thing to do is to fill in our list, this is done using the append function, in the numbers variable, which, if you remember is an empty list, after it is filled in, it already becomes a list with integer values as items.

We are already able to filter the list, and we do it creating a list called pairs, which will use the filter function, and the same one will return the values of the arrangement that the function returns to us as True, as for example 2, since this one is higher than zero and the module of the division of the same one, between two is equal to zero, therefore, it fulfills the requirements.

The last step is to print in screen all the obtained pairs, and we do it with the help of another cycle for, in which a variable x, will iterate through all the list and will print us that those numbers are even.

Function map()

The map() function is the one that is in charge of executing each element on a list or tuple to be able to return a sequence of elements which will be the result of the operation.

```python
def sum(a, b):
    return a + b

list1=[1, 0, 1, 0, 1]
list2=[0, 2, 0, 2, 0]
c=map(sum, list1, list2)
print(list(c))

string1=["Hello, ", "are "]
string2=["how ","you"]
c=map(sum, string1, string2)
print(list(c))
```

In this example, we can see in the first lines, the definition of a function called sum, which has as parameters, variables a and b do not have to be exclusively integers, they can be strings or any other type of data. It will return a+b, whether it is a concatenation or a sum.

Later, we created two lists, the "List1" and the "List2", the same, are lists that have within them, an iteration of numbers between one and zero, this is for List1, now for the case two it is analogous, but in this case, are iterations between the numbers two and zero.

Then, we declare a variable c, it will make use of the map function, and will receive as arguments, the function sum, list1, and list2, what this will do is to create a list that will be in a specific memory address, which will have as items, the sum of list1 and list2. To print what is in c, it is important to use the list() sentence, since if you want to show the desired data, we have to tell the program that we want to see the list that is in that memory address.

Later, two variables were defined, the first is string1 and the second is string2, which will have a message. After the declarations, the map variable is used, and it receives the parameters sum, string1 and string2, what we are doing in this case, is concatenating the strings that there are as item of each list. Finally, we will print in screen the value of the list that is in the address c.

What are the differences between the lambda functions and the functions defined with "def" sentence?

We know that functions created with the lambda function can also be created with the "def" statement. What does this mean? This means nothing more than creating a function with either of these two statements is considered a correct action. This is because by both methods you can get the same result, with simpler options.

We can see this as a path, both reach the same destination, the difference is that one is longer and heavier and another is much simpler, as that is the lambda function used for, to make it easier to use functions in our code.

When we create a lambda type function, it will only focus on using a single line of code, thus minimizing the number of lines that can be used in a code, unlike the def statement, which usually occupies many times more than one line of code.

When using the lambda keyword, we create an object or function which is not going to have the need to be defined with a name, unlike the def statement which must be defined at the beginning of the program so that it can interpret it.

Although using the lambda function is much simpler for the code, many times the def statement is more understandable for those users who are starting as programmers and even for those users who have programming knowledge but not so much experience.

It is of fundamental need that at the moment of operating with the lambda function, this one is assigned a variable since if this is not done, the same one is going to operate only in the line in which it is going to be defined.

Chapter 6: Object-Oriented Programming-OOP

At this level, we are already able to design the program based on functions, so that we are able to use statements that manipulate the data. In this programming language, we can find procedure-oriented programming and object-oriented programming, which uses types defined by the programmer to organize both codes and data.

What is OOP and what are its advantages?

It is a form of programming used by modern languages, which consists of transferring the behavior that objects have in real life to the programming code. It is a way of organizing your program combining data and functionality by wrapping it in something called an object. Some of the programming languages that use this object-oriented paradigm are Python, C++, Java, Visual, etc.

As advantages we can mention the following:

- We can divide the programs into pieces, parts, modules or classes to this concept in programming are called modularization.

- It is a code that can be reusable, unlike what happens with procedure-oriented programming, so, if we get to create an application with this object-oriented program and later want to make another similar application we can reuse this code. Now in order to be able to reuse the code of one application in another, we have to know and understand the concept of "inheritance".

- If there is a fault in any line of code, the program continues to work, it is likely that the line of code that generated the error will not perform the intended task, but the rest of the program will.

- Encapsulation.

Object-oriented programming is responsible for applying programming techniques such as:

a. Abstraction: Abstraction refers to the process of design and interpretation, which focuses on recognizing the important characteristics of an object; thus filtering out and ignoring the particularities that will not be considered important.

Abstraction focuses on defining the characteristics of an object, which distinguish it from other types. It focuses on what it is, not what it does, and then specifies what it should be implemented in.

For example: We are going to apply abstraction to flowers.
Object: Flowers
Characteristics
- Colors
- Leaves
- Nectar
- Roots
Functionalities:
- Production of seeds and fruits
- Pollination
- Reproduction

b. Inheritance: some objects share the same properties and methods as other objects, and also add new properties and methods. We call this inheritance, a class that inherits from another, as happens in real life when in a family group one of the children inherits the skin color of one of the parents, he would be inheriting or having their own characteristics or properties, but also one in common with one of their parents, the same happens in programming.

What does this mean? In a simpler way we can say that when we create a new class, we can implement the same data of the base class. This new class will have more specific data than the original class, which contains a more general view.

In Python, when a class does not inherit another, it must be inherited from an object, which is the main Python class that defines an object.

Once an object has been created, or once the class instance has been made, it is possible to access its method and properties and for that Python uses a very simple syntax which is, the name of the object, followed by the point and the property or the method to which you want to access.

Python also supports a limited form of multiple inheritances.

Types of inheritance:

- Basic Inheritance: This occurs when a class inherits only one base class.

- Multiple inheritance: This occurs when a class inherits two or more base classes.

- Polymorphism: Refers to those different behaviors, which are associated with objects that are different, but may share the same name. When you call an object by its name (which has several objects), its behavior will be based on the object you are currently using.

Types of polymorphism:

- Parametric polymorphism: Parametric polymorphism is the one that allows functions and classes to be written in a generic way, in this way the data of the same can be manipulated without taking into account its type.

- Polymorphism of subtypes: The polymorphism of subtypes is the one in which the subtypes of a type (class) allow to substitute the behavior of the functions of the original type with an own implementation.

- Ad Hoc Polymorphism: Ad Hoc polymorphism refers to those functions, which vary their behavior according to the type of arguments they receive.

What is the terminology or vocabulary that we are going to use in OOP?

We will mention the most commonly used vocabulary to better understand this code:

- Class: Classes are models on which objects are built, that is, models where the common characteristics of a group of objects are written. To better understand this term we will do it by means of analogies, for example, if we have a car, the class would be the chassis and the wheels, since it is a common characteristic among the group of objects that are the cars. If we want to create a Python application that builds cars, the first thing we have to do is to create a class that defines what are the common characteristics of the cars we want to make and this class must have defined within it the construction of a chassis and the construction of four wheels.

In this case, to see another abstraction, let's show an example of classes, but in this case, the class will be a house.

```
class.py        ×

1       class house():
2           color="red"
3           dors=6
4           kitchen=True
5           bathroom=3
6           levels=2
7
8       house1=house()
9       print("We create a house")
```

As we can see in the example, the first thing to do is to declare that house is a class, using the reserved word class. Within it, it has some attributes, such as that the color is red, it has six doors, that it does have a kitchen, it has three bathrooms and two floors.

Now the next step is to create a variable and convert it as a class, for it, any name is placed and then the same is entered the name of the class and parentheses. As you can see in the example, house1 is an object, which has a house class and has all the attributes previously explained.

Finally, to know if the class has been created well, a print is made in the console to verify the proper functioning of the program.

- Exemplar of class, which is the same as to speak of the instance of class, and of object belonging to a class, which means that, exemplar, instance and object of class are synonyms; an instance would be an object or exemplar belonging to a class. For example, following with the automobile, we have already talked about that the class defines the characteristics that are common to it, and that define the objects that we are going to use, and we have seen that the class is formed in our example by the chassis and the wheels, but the objects that belong to that class could be different models of automobiles, that share a common characteristic that is to have the same chassis (it should be noted that there are cars that despite belonging to other brands are assembled with identical chassis) and four wheels, so we can have two cars with their own characteristics that are defined within the object itself (the car), such as color, model, weight, seats, steering wheel, then we could say that a specific car is an object belonging to the class, an exemplar of class or that is an instance of class; and another car of another brand would be another different object belonging to the same class, a different instance of the same class, or a different exemplar of the same class.

- Modularization; When we create a complex application applied to objects such as Python, for example, the most normal is that this application is composed of several classes, not a single class, which can also occur, but the normal is that if the application is complex it will be composed of several classes, the concept of modularization derives from an application can be composed of several classes, for example, applying it to real objects, if we imagine an old sound system, they were made up of several modules, the corresponding to the cassette, equalizer, radio, and disk, which means that the object was made up of several modules. These modules have the advantage to work in an independent way, that is to say, when the radio was damaged, we could use the module of cassette, in programming this leads to an advantage, if you have a program written in Python divided in modules and one of the classes for any reason fails the most probable thing is that the program continues working, just that the class in which you have problems will not be able to carry out its task as with the analogy of the sound equipment.

- Encapsulation; the functioning of a complete class of our object-oriented program is encapsulated, that means that the other classes do not handle any information about each other; going back to the analogy of the previous sound equipment, if we take the equalizer module of the sound equipment, the internal functioning of the equalizer corresponds only to the equalizer, meaning the functioning of the cassette module, nothing knows or understands the equalizer module, and that is what is known as encapsulation. Somehow all the classes are connected so that they function as equipment, but at the same time, each of the classes is encapsulated so that the internal functioning of that class is not accessible from outside. The different parts of a program are connected so that they form part of a team with something called access methods. Creating access methods we get to connect one class with another so that they work as a unit or a team, but these access methods will only have access to certain characteristics of each of the classes. You can access from one class to another so that they are connected to each other, but there are certain characteristics of each of the classes that are encapsulated so that they are not accessible

How do we build classes, objects, and how do we access the properties and characteristics of an object in Python?

To access the properties and characteristics of an object we use what is known as nomenclature of the point, commonly used in object-oriented programming, to explain what it is, we will do it based on an example.

Suppose that we have given our object a name, we call it myCar, all objects, instances or exemplars must have a name, in order to access the properties of the car in our program we use the nomenclature of the point:
E.g. Syntax: Name of the object. Property = New Value
myCar.color="red"

This is the syntax in the case of Python that we have to follow if we want to access the property of the object, we use the nomenclature of the point. To access the behavior of the object from the code, we also use the nomenclature of the point.

E.g. Syntax: Object name.behavior

    myCar.starts()

    myCar.stops()

In the following example, you will learn how to access the attributes of a class, through the nomenclature of the point, so you can understand better.

```
class.py    ×

1    class house():
2        color="red"
3        doors=6
4        kitchen=True
5        bathroom=3
6        levels=2
7
8    house1=house()
9    print("The house color is "+house1.color+", have "+str(house1.dors)+" doors")
10   print("The house have "+str(house1.levels)+" levels, and "+str(house1.bathroom)+" bathrooms")
```

The first thing we see in this example is the creation of the house class, which has its attributes, like the color, which in this case is red, the doors that have six, or the floors that have two.

Then, we can see how we create our house1 instance, which is of the house type. But we do not only want to stay with the creation of the class, but we also want to access the data that these have, therefore we will make a screen print of the attributes that the house has, as you can see, what we proceed to do, is to concatenate the string that we have written, and concatenate it with the attribute we want, now, to access to it, we have to name the instance, and through the nomenclature of the point, the attribute we want to access.

Now we are going to talk about how to build a code of what a class is; being the class the base to later be able to create objects, examplers or instances that belong to that class.

```
class.py        ×

1    class obj():
2            <statement 1>
3            .
4            .
5            .
6            .
7            .
8            <statement n>
9
10   a=obj()
11
```

This, more than an example, is an explanation of the syntax to the declaration of a class, because, although we sound repetitive, the declaration of them, is something fundamental in the programming oriented to objects, because as already you must suppose, it is the basis. Therefore, the first thing is to make the statement of the class nameobject():, with this, we are creating a class, which is named nameobject. Then, inside it, there is a cumulus of statements, which are responsible for giving value to the attributes of the instances and to work with the methods, which will be explained later.

There are cases in which you will ask yourself, but all the houses are red or all the plants have three leaves? And well, obviously the answer is no, for that we are going to work with the builders, they will allow us to give uniqueness to the instances. These are methods, but it is not too much to say since now that these are the ones that allow us to give different values to each instance, at the moment of initializing them, we will see them later.

Although you should already know what an attribute is, since we have worked with them previously in this chapter, we will now proceed to explain them formally.

Attribute:
We define attributes as those values that variables possess within each object. What do we mean by this? Let's

imagine the case of a classroom in a school; an attribute that each classroom may possess is the grade the students are in or the age of them.

The word attribute can be used for anything after a point, for example, if we have the expression, z.real, real is an attribute of the object z, what we had previously called as the nomenclature of the point.

The attributes can be read-only, or write-only. In this last case, the assignment to attributes is possible. The attributes of a module can be written: module. the_answer = 42, these attributes can also be deleted when desired with the instruction del. As, for example: del module.the_answer, will eliminate the attribute the_answer of the object with module name.

```
class.py    ×

1    class house():
2        color="red"
3        dors=6
4        kitchen=True
5        bathroom=3
6        levels=2
7
8    house1=house()
9    house1.color="green"
10   print(house1.color)
11
```

The first thing we do in this example is the definition of the class house(), and within it, we define each attribute of the same, like color, bathroom, kitchen, among others.

The next step is the creation of the house1 instance, which is of the house type, as you may have expected, but if you want to paint the house, we will proceed to access the attribute, by means of the instruction house1.color = "green" in this way, the color has been changed from house1 to "green".

To make sure that the color has been changed correctly, a screen print of the color attribute of the house1 instance is made using the nomenclature of the dot.

Methods:

Since we have seen that each object has certain attributes that have certain specific behaviors; now we will call methods to each function created within each class. How is this? So let's go back to the last example of the classroom, it has two methods or actions which are to study and attend classes.

To create a method we use the word def, that we already know, but when we write it, there is a keyword that we cannot forget, which is a parameter of the method, this word is self, and this one is used to be able to access to the attributes of the class. We can observe that there is a difference between method and function and is that a method is a special function that belongs to the class being created, while a function does not belong to any class.

The characteristics of a method are the reserved word called def, name of the function, a default parameter called self.

Often, the first argument of the method is called self. this is nothing more than a convention; the name self means nothing to Python, in the sense that it is indifferent to put this as first or last parameter (because the position does not matter, but yes or yes it has to be the word self), but if you do not follow this convention your code could be less readable to other Python programmers.

If the concept of what attributes are, has been well understood, we will be able to observe that working with the methods is very simple, only that when working with them, we have to take into account that means to add behavior to objects, so that you can change attributes when accessing a method or return some value.

```python
class house():
    color="red"
    dors=6
    kitchen=True
    bathroom=3
    levels=2

    def open(self):
        print("The door is open")
house1=house()
house1.color="White"
print(house1.color)
house1.open()
```

In this example, we see again, how to create the class house, but it differs from the others because it has created a different method, called open, as you can see, it makes use of the sentence def, then we will put the name of the method, then, within some parentheses, place the parameters, always, but always we must place the self as parameters, you can also add others, but the self can not miss. After this, it is treated as a normal function, as you can see, the method is responsible for sending a message, which communicates that the door is open.

Later you can see how to create the instance house1, which is class house, one of the actions that are done on house1, is to change the color of it, the new color is white, another important action is access to the methods, and as you can see, it is also done through the nomenclature of the dot.

Constructors:

Now that you have basic knowledge of classes, you should ask yourself if all the instances of one class are the same as the others, because if this were true, everything would be very monotonous, and the OOP would not be very powerful, as it really is, for this reason, the constructors have been created, which initialize the classes with values that the programmer wants.

A constructor, is the one that creates or assigns values to the initial attributes of an instance, and to do this, it is necessary to use a method, moreover, a constructor is a method of a class, to use it, we make use of the reserved word __init__(self, a, b, c, ...), being a, b, c, the parameters that we want to initialize, since they are values that we can introduce as users and thus be able to assign the values to the attributes, in order to achieve diversity in our objects.

```python
class house():
    def __init__(self, color, dors, kitchen, bathroom, levels):
        self.color=color
        self.dors=dors
        self.kitchen=kitchen
        self.bathroom=bathroom
        self.levels=levels

    def open(self):
        print("The door is open")

    def paint(self, c):
        self.color=c
house1=house("blue", 5, True, 2, 1)
print(house1.color)
house1.paint("black")
print(house1.color)
house1.open()
```

In this example, we can already see how things change and become more fun, the first thing is that a constructor was used, the same has as parameters the self, color, doors, kitchen, among others. After the constructor's statement we use the word self and place the corresponding value, as you can see between lines three and seven, for example, in the instruction of line 3, what is said is that the variable color of that specific instance, is going to have the value, what the argument has valued when the instance was initialized.

Then you can see how the open method was created, that method, only shows on screen that the door has been opened; the other method that has been created, in this case, is one called paint, which is responsible for changing the color of that instance, this was done using the sentence self.color, to specify that the instance is going to change.

Subsequently, the house1 instance is created, and it is given as argument "blue", 5, True, 2, 1 to the constructor so that he initializes his attributes in those specific values and thus to be able to remove the monotony that we had before.

After having created the instance, the color of the house is printed in screen, or well, better said, of the house1 instance, at this moment, it should print the string "blue", then, it makes use of the paint method, to change the color of the instance, to the black color, to verify that the color has been changed correctly, the color of the house1 instance is printed in screen, and for this case, the string "black" should appear in console.

Finally, the open method is used, so that it appears on the screen that the doors are open.

Since we know how to make use of the builders, we can apply the concept of inheritance previously applied, so that a class related to it, inherits, behaviors and attributes of its parent class.

```python
class house():
    def __init__(self, color, dors, kitchen, bathroom, levels):
        self.color=color
        self.dors=dors
        self.kitchen=kitchen
        self.bathroom=bathroom
        self.levels=levels

    def open(self):
        print("The door is open")

    def paint(self, c):
        self.color=c
class apartment(house):
    def __init__(self, color, dors, kitchen, bathroom, levels, stairs, elevator):
        house.__init__(self, color, dors, kitchen, bathroom, levels)
        self.stairs=stairs
        self.elevator=elevator
    def elevatoron(self):
        if(self.elevator==True):
            print("The elevator is in PB")
        else:
            print("You dont have elevator")
house1=house("blue", 5, True, 2, 1)
print(house1.color)
house1.paint("black")
print(house1.color)
house1.open()
apartment1=apartment("orange", 2, True, 2, 1, True, True)
apartment1.elevatoron()
apartment1.open()
```

In this example, we can see how inheritance works, since we have already seen the first lines of the code, it is not necessary to explain them in-depth, since what we do is create the house class, initialize the house constructor and create some methods such as paint and open.

Then, we define the second class, which is apartment. Why do we say that it is a daughter of house class? Well, we already know that an apartment is a house, but a house doesn't have to be an apartment, it can be a mansion or a townhouse, therefore it doesn't have to be an apartment, whereas in the opposite case, that is always true.

As we can see, at the moment of defining the apartment class, we enter as parameter, the parent class, in this case, house. Then we start the constructor, which should have the word reserved __init__, and put the parameters self and all that those that are missing, with this we mean both the parameters of entry of the class house, plus the additional ones of the class apartment, as it can be stairs, and elevator, since the apartments can have stairs or not, in an analogical way it is done with the elevators. They must be initialized as well. Later, as we can see, we will call the function of constructors of the parent class, so that the same ones are initialized, using the nomenclature of the dot, then, it is when the other attributes that are not in house, like stairs or elevator were initialized. A method that was created within the apartment class, was the elevatoron() which, depending on whether the instance created has an apartment or not, when calling this method, will appear on screen that the elevator is on the ground floor.

Already after having created all the classes, we proceed to create the instances, to verify that the classes were created correctly, in a similar way to how the object house1 was created, this one is created, with the same values of the previous example, the color of the object is printed, then the function paint() is used, and the color is changed to black, and finally the door is opened. Then, the other object that creates the apartment1, which has as arguments the orange color, two doors, True on kitchen, two baths, one floor, stairs and also has elevator. In the program is called the function elevatoron() to call the elevator and reach the ground floor, and show the user that this in PB, then proceeds to open the doors of the apartment with the help of the open method.

As we can see, object-oriented programming is extremely useful, since it allows us to see the problems of programming as problems of real-life and make solutions as if they were objects with which we run into in everyday life, for that reason, we strongly recommend programming this way, as it reduces the number of lines to use, and makes the code reusable, in addition to being more understandable.

Chapter 7: Modules

The modules are files with extension .py (that we have been using until now), additionally a module instead of having extension py, it also has the extension .pyc; (what would be a compiled Python file), a module can also be a file written totally in C for those that are using CPython.

Modules have their own namespace, and in addition, they can contain variables, functions, classes and even contain other modules, a module within another or a submodule.

How useful are the modules?

The modules are mainly used to organize and reuse the code, this leads us to two terms that are fundamental in OOP as are modularization and reuse.

When we want to make a complex application and we need a code to reuse it since it was previously programmed in another application, this is one of the advantages that modules have, they allow us to reuse our code in different applications.

The modularization, in this case, we divide the module in codes, in small parts, when we realize a complex application, we can do it in a single file of thousands of lines of code, or we can divide it in small parts, in small files with a smaller number of lines of codes since it is always going to be easier for us to handle.

How can we create a module in Python?

We can easily create a module through the file extension .py, once created the file we can save it where we want, this is what we know as import.

Python provides us with a large number of modules in its standard library, in the official Python manual we can find this library through the following link: http://docs.python.org/modindex.html.

Inside a module, its name is available in the value of the global variable _name_.

Import Sentence

A module can contain executable statements and function definitions; with these statements, we are able to initialize the module. They are executed only the first time the module is in an import statement.

Modules can import other modules. It is actually usual to place all import declarations at the beginning of the module (or script, for that matter). The names of the imported modules will be placed in the global namespace of the importing module.

The import sentence has the following syntax

Once the interpreter finds the import statement, it will import the module if it is present in the search path, where a search path is nothing more than a list of directories that the interpreter searches for before importing a module.

Chapter 8: File handling

The Python programming language allows us to work on two different levels when we refer to file systems and directories. One of them is through the module os, which facilitates us to work with the whole system of files and directories, at the level of the operating system itself.

The second level is the one that allows us to work with files, this is done by manipulating their reading and writing at the application level, and treating each file as an object.

In python as well as in any other language, the files are manipulated in three steps, first they are opened, then they are operated on or edited and finally they are closed.

What is a file?

A python file is a set of bytes, which are composed of a structure, and within this we find in the header, where all the data of the file is handled such as, for example, the name, size and type of file we are working with; the data is part of the body of the file, where the written content is handled by the editor and finally the end of the file, where we notify the code through this sentence that we reach the end of the file. In this way, we can describe the structure of a file.

The structure of the files is composed in the following way:

- File header: These are the data that the file will contain (name, size, type)
- File Data: This will be the body of the file and will have some content written by the programmer.
- End of file: This sentence is the one that will indicate that the file has reached its end.

Our file will look like this:

**Header of file
(name, size, type)**

Body of file (data)

End of file

How can I access a file?

There are two very basic ways to access a file, one is to use it as a text file, where you proceed line by line, the other is to treat it as a binary file, where you proceed byte by byte.

Now, to assign a variable a file type value, we will need to use the function open (), which will allow us to open a file.

Open() function

To open a file in Python, we have to use the open() function, since this will receive the name of the file and the way in which the file will be opened as parameters. If the file opening mode is not entered, it will open in the default way in a read-only file.

We must keep in mind that the operations to open the files are limited because it is not possible to read a file that was opened only for writing, you cannot write to a file which has been opened only for reading.

The open () function consists of two parameters:
- It is the path to the file we want to open.
- It is the mode in which we can open it.
Its syntax is as follows:

```
1    function = open("file.txt", "w")
2    function.write()
3    function.close()
```

Of which the parameters:

File: This is an argument that provides the name of the file we want to access with the open() function, this is what will be the path of our file.

The argument file is considered a fundamental argument, since it is the main one (allowing us to open the file), unlike the rest of the arguments which can be optional and have values that are already predetermined.

Mode: The access modes are those that are in charge of defining the way in which the file is going to be opened (it could be for reading, writing, editing).

There are a variety of access modes, these are:

r	This is the default open mode. Opens the file for reading only
r+	This mode opens the file for its reading and writing

rb	This mode opens the file for reading only in a binary format
w	This mode opens the file for writing only. In case the file does not exist, this mode creates it
w+	This is similar to the w mode, but this allows the file to be read
wb	This mode is similar to the w mode, but this opens the file in a binary format
wb+	This mode is similar to the wb mode, but this allows the file to be read
a	This mode opens a file to be added. The file starts writing from the end
ab	This is similar to mode a, but opens the file in a binary format
a+	This mode is pretty much like the mode a, but allows us to read the file.

In summary, we have three letters, or three main modes: r,w and a. And two submodes, + and b.

In Python, there are two types of files: Text files and plain files. It is very important to specify in which format the file will be opened to avoid any error in our code.

Read a file:

There are three ways to read a file:

1. read([n])

2. readlines()

3. readline([n])

Surely at this point, we have the question of what is meant by the letter n enclosed in parentheses and square brackets? It's very simple, the letter n is going to notify the bytes that the file is going to read and interpret.

Read method ([ ])

```
1   myfile = open("D:\\pythonfile\\mypythonfile.txt","r")
2   myfile.read(9)
```

There we could see that inside the read() there is a number 9, which will tell Python that he has to read only the first nine letters of the file

Readline(n) Method

The readline method is the one that reads a line from the file, so that the read bytes can be returned in the form of a string. The readline method is not able to read more than one line of code, even if the byte n exceeds the line quantity.

Its syntax is very similar to the syntax of the read() method.

```
1    myfile = open("D:\\pythonfile\\mypythonfile.txt","r")
2    myfile.readline()
```

Readlines(n) Method

The readlines method is the one that reads all the lines of the file, so that the read bytes can be taken up again in the form of a string. Unlike the readline method, this one is able to read all the lines.

Like the read() method and readline() its syntax are very similar:

```
1    myfile = open("D:\\pythonfile\\mypythonfile.txt","r")
2    myfile.readlines()
```

Once we have opened a file, there are many types of information (attributes) we could get to know more about our files. These attributes are:

File.name: This is an attribute that will return the name of the file.

File.mode: This is an attribute that will return the accesses with which we have opened a file.

file.closed: This is an attribute that will return a "True" if the file we were working with is closed and if the file we were working with is still open, it will return a "False".

Close() function

The close function is the method by which any type of information that has been written in the memory of our program is eliminated, in order to proceed to close the file. But that is not the only way to close a file; we can also do it when we reassign an object from one file to another file.

The syntax of the close function is as follows:

What's a buffer?

We can define the buffer as a file which is given a temporary use in the ram memory; this will contain a fragment of data that composes the sequence of files in our operating system. We use buffers very often when we work with a file which we do not know the storage size.

It is important to keep in mind that, if the size of the file were to exceed the ram memory that our equipment has, its processing unit will not be able to execute the program and work correctly.

What is the size of a buffer for? The size of a buffer is the one that will indicate the available storage space while we use the file. Through the function: io.DEFAULT_BUFFER_SIZE the program will show us the size of our file in the platform in a predetermined way.

We can observe this in a clearer way:

```python
import io
    print("Default buffer size:"io.DEFAULT_BUFFER_SIZE)
    file= open("Myfile.txt", mode= "r", buffering=6)
    print(file.line_buffering)
file_contents=file.buffer
for line in file_contents
    print(line)
```

Errors

In our files, we are going to find a string (of the optional type) which is going to specify the way in which we could handle the coding errors in our program.

Errors can only be used in txt mode files.

These are the following:

Ignore_errors()	This will avoid the comments with a wrong or unknown format
Strict_errors()	This is going to generate a subclass or UnicodeError in case that any mistake or fail comes out in our code file

Encoding

The string encoding is frequently used when we work with data storage and this is nothing more than the representation of the encoding of characters, whose system is based on bits and bytes as a representation of the same character.

This is expressed as follows:

```
1    string.encode(encoding="UTF-8", errors= "strict")
2
```

Newline

The Newline mode is the one that is going to control the functionalities of the new lines, which can be '\r', " ", none, '\n', and '\r\n'.

The newlines are universal and can be seen as a way of interpreting the text sequences of our code.

1.   The end-of-line sentence in Windows: "\r\n".
2.   The end-of-line sentence in Max Os: "\r".
3.   The end-of-line sentence in UNIX: "\n"

On input: If the newline is of the None type, the universal newline mode is automatically activated.

Input lines can end in "\r", "\n" or "\r\n" and are automatically translated to "\n" before being returned by our program. If their respective legal parameters when coding are met, the entry of the lines will end only by the same given string and their final line will not be translated at the time of return.

On output: If the newline is of the None type, any type of character "\n" that has been written, will be translated to a line separator which we call "os.linesep".

If the newline is of the type " " no type of translator is going to be made, and in case the newline meets any value of which are considered the legal for the code, they will be automatically translated to the string.

Example of newline reading for " ".

```
1    string.encode(mode="r", newline= " ")
2
```

Example of newline reading for none:

```
1    string.encode(mode="w", newline= "none")
2
```

Manage files through the "os" module

The "os" module allows us to perform certain operations, these will depend on an operating system (actions such as starting a process, listing files in a folder, end process and others).

There are a variety of methods with the "os" module which allow us to manage files, these are:

os.makedirs()	This method of the "os" module will create a new file
os.path.getsize()	This method of the "os" module will show the size of a file in bytes.
os.remove(file_name)	This method of the "os" module will delete a file or the program
os.getcwd ()	This method of the "os" module will show us the actual directory from where we will be working
os.listdir()	This method of the "os" module will list all the content of any folder of our file
os.rename (current_new)	This method of the "os" module will rename a file
os.path.isdir()	This method of the "os" module will transfer the parameters of the program to a folder
os.chdir()	This method of the "os" module will change or update the direction of any folder or directory

os.path.isfile()	This method of the "os" module will transform a parameter into a file.

Xlsx files: xlsx files are those files in which you work with spreadsheets, how is this? Well, this is nothing more than working with programs like Excel. For example, if we have the windows operating system on our computer, we have the advantage that when working with this type of files, the weight of it will be much lighter than other types of files.

The xlsx type files are very useful when working with databases, statistics, calculations, numerical type data, graphics and even certain types of basic automation.

In this chapter we are going to learn to work the basic functionalities of this type of files, this includes creating files, opening files and modifying files.

To start this, first we will have to install the necessary library; we do this by executing the command "pip3 install openpyxl" in our Python terminal.

Once executed this command it is going to download and install the openpyxl module in our Python files, we can also look for documentation to get the necessary information about this module.

Create an xlsx file: To create a file with this module, let's use the openpyxl() Workbook() function.

```
1    from openpyxl import Workbook
2    def xlsxdoc():
3        wb = Workbook()
4        sheet = wb.active
5        name = "test.xlsx"
6        wb.save(name)
7    xlsxdoc()
```

This is the first step that we will do to manage the files of the type xlsx, we can see that first we have created the file importing the function Workbook of the module openpyxl; followed by this to the variable wb we have assigned the function Workbook() with this we declare that this will be the document with which we are going to work (we create the object in the form of a worksheet in this format). Once this is done, we activate the object whose name is wb in order to assign it a name and finally save the file.

Add information to the file with this module:

In order to add information to our file, we will need to use another type of functions that come included with the object, one of them is the append function.

```
1    from openpyxl import Workbook
2    def xlsxaoc():
3        wb = Workbook()
4        sheet = wb.active
5        sheet = ["B4"] = "Goodnight"
6        name = "test.xlsx"
7        wb.save(name)
8    xlsxdoc()
```

We can observe that this is similar to the last example that we needed to create a document, for it we did the usual steps: we created in the function xlsxdoc() the object wb, we activated the object and there we added the information. In this new space we will need to know the specific position in which we are going to write, in this case, we will write in the fourth box of the second row "B4" and these will be matched with a string that says "goodnight". The final steps are exactly the same as the last example, therefore, we will place the name and save it with the save command.

There is a simpler way to write and enter data, we can do this through the function append()

```
1   from openpyxl import Workbook
2   def xlsxdoc():
3       wb = Workbook()
4       sheet = wb.active
5       messages = ("Hello" , "good morning", "goodnight" )
6       sheet,append = (messages)
7       name = "test.xlsx"
8       wb.save(name)
9   xlsxdoc()
```

We can observe that we have created the document "test.xlsx" with the steps that we explained previously, we can observe that we have created a tuple called messages, this tuple has three items that are:

"Hello", "goodmorning", "goodnight".

Once the tuple is created, we use the append function, which will allow us to attach all the information contained in the tuple messages and finally save the document with the save function.

The append() function only admits iterable data, what does this mean? This refers to the data of type arrangements, tuples since, if they are not entered in this way, our program will return an error.

Read documents in xlsx

```python
1    from openpyxl import Workbook
2    name = "test.xlsx"
3    def xlsxdoc():
4        wb = load_Workbook(name)
5        sheet = wb.active
6        file1 = sheet["C1"].value
7        file2 = sheet["C2"].value
8        file3 = sheet["C3"].value
9        print(file1)
10       print(file2)
11       print(file3)
12   xlsxdoc()
```

Let's go back to our first example to get information from xlsx files, we could see that, for this, we imported the load_workbook class. The first thing we need to know is the name of the file we want to open and for this, we created the variable with the name.

It is important that the files are located in the same folder in which the program is stored, because otherwise the program will throw us an error. Inside the function xlsdoc() we will create the object wb that will be with which we are going to work, followed by this the object "sheet" is created which is going to represent the sheet that we are going to use.

Once all this is done, we are going to request the information of the specific boxes "C1", "C2", "C3" next to the function value, to validate that the information that we acquire is real, we print all the information requested.

Handling PDF files

It is known that the initials of this type of file are: "Portable Document Format", which have grown significantly over the years, are mostly used in business and education. This is due to the fact that they provide a great amount of benefits in which its security is highlighted, allowing to add access keys to control who can edit the document and even add a watermark to it to avoid plagiarism of information.

Other outstanding data is that these documents can be seen from any device since it is not necessary to have a specific program; in addition, the weight of the files is much lower since these texts are compressed, unlike Word documents.

A disadvantage of PDF files could be that they are not easy to edit once they have been created.

In this chapter, we will only learn how to create PDF files.

To create a PDF file the first thing we will have to do is to download the library through the command "Pip3 install fpdf", followed by this we can proceed to create our document:

```
1    from fpdf import FPDF
2
3    pdfdoc = PDF()
4    pdfdoc.set_font('Times New Roman', 'B', 12)
5    pdfdoc.add_page()
6    pdfdoc.cell(12, 10, "First PDF program", 5, 6, "C")
7    pdfdoc.output("first PDF", 'F')
```

This is a simple level example, but at the same time, it is much more difficult than other types of files. To start a document you need a lot of commands, for it we will import the FPDF class from the fpdf library, followed by this we create the pdfdoc object and this will be the pdf document. Once created this document, we will have to customize the formats, size, and style of the letters we are going to use. To do this we use the command set_font.

In this case, the type of Font that we are going to use is going to be Times New Roman, with bold style and a size of 12.

Followed by this we will add a page through the command add_page(), since we will need a page on which to write and the function fpdf does not create a blank page by default. Then, we're going to insert information with the cell() function which contains a set of very important arguments.

The cell function will contain the width and height that the cell will occupy, it must include the message that will be written in string format, in case it is required that the edges to come with some detail included we must add 1 since the 0 is by default and does not allow anything to be inserted.

If you want to add a cell below or located to the right, you place a 0 and otherwise is placed 1, if you want the text to be centered to the right, left, up or down a string will be placed and if you want in it to be centered you write C

Finally, we will have to save the document through the command output(), and the arguments that will go with them will be the name of the file (with the ".pdf" included since we want a file in pdf) and then a string "F".

Managing BIN files

As we saw earlier, not all files are necessarily text files. These same ones can be processed by lines and even there exist certain files that when being processed, each byte contains a particular meaning for the program; for that reason, they need to be manipulated in their specific format.

A clear example of this are the files in Binary, to work with this type of files is no more than adding a b in the space of the parameter mode.

For example:

```
1   with open("pythonfile", "rb") as f:
2       byte = f.read(4)
3       while byte:
4           byte = f.read(4)
```

When we handle a binary file, it is very important to know the current position of the data we need in order to modify it. If you don't know the current position, the file.tell() function will indicate the number of bytes that have elapsed since we started the file.

In case you want to modify the current position in the file, we use the function file.seek(star, from) which will allow us to move a certain amount of bytes from start to finish.

Conclusion

Thank you for making it through to the end of *Python programming for beginners: The ultimate crash course to learn python computer language faster and easier,* we really hope that you found it informative and that you were able to approach all of the tools here provided that you needed to achieve your goals of learning Python programming language

Now that you have finished this book, you should be able to do a lot of programs for different situations. The next step is to keep practicing a lot, in order to become a master of Python. While programming, sometimes you might think that some things are impossible to code, or that you are not good enough to do them. But that is not right; you just have to think a lot in order to make it happen. Also while programming you may find that your code or program is not working, do not worry, even the smartest people write codes that do not work at the beginning. You just have to keep trying.

As you know, nowadays technology is everywhere and so programming is, our recommendation is that you try to code and solve problems of your daily activities in order to broaden your vision of the world since all electronics have hundreds and hundreds of lines of codes on it.

Good luck with programming!!

```
if: (you_have_doubts)
        print("Read_The_Book_Again")
else:
        print("GOODBYE")
```

www.ingramcontent.com/pod-product-compliance
Lightning Source LLC
LaVergne TN
LVHW051221050326
832903LV00028B/2200